OUR LIVING WORLD OF NATURE

The
Life
of the
African
Plains

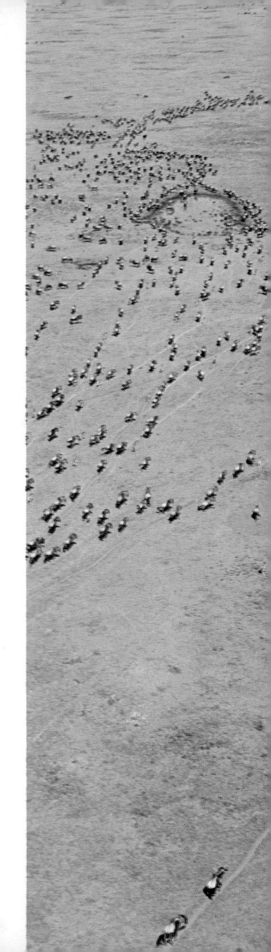

Developed jointly with The World Book Encyclopedia

OUR LIVING WORLD OF NATURE

The
Life
of the
African
Plains

LESLIE BROWN

Published in cooperation with
The World Book Encyclopedia

McGraw-Hill Book Company
NEW YORK   TORONTO   LONDON

LESLIE BROWN, *a long-time resident of Africa, was formerly Chief Agriculturist for Kenya. His responsibilities in that position were extensive, including supervision of agricultural development, range management, and irrigation schemes. Upon retirement in 1963 he was awarded the Order of the British Empire for services to agriculture. At that time Mr. Brown developed a special interest in Ethiopia and has since conducted and organized several expeditions to remote areas in order to ascertain the status of threatened wildlife. A naturalist with wide-ranging interests, he is a world-renowned authority on the ecology of African wildlife. Besides serving a term as president of the East African Natural History Society, he is a member of the East African Wildlife Society and a number of other conservation organizations. He is the author of* Africa: A Natural History, African Birds of Prey, Ethiopian Episode, *and several other books, as well as countless scientific papers and popular magazine articles. At present Leslie Brown is a visiting Professor of Research at the Faculty of Science of the University of Addis Ababa, and a special consultant on range research for the Ford Foundation.*

Library of Congress Cataloging in Publication Data

Brown, Leslie.
  The life of the African plains.

  (Our living world of nature)
  1. Grassland ecology—Africa. 2. Savannas
—Africa. 3. Natural history—Africa. I. Title.
QH541.5.P7B76   574.5'264   74-177589
ISBN 0-07-008245-6
ISBN 0-07-046013-2 (sub. ed.)

12345678910 NR RM 78765432

OUR LIVING WORLD OF NATURE

Contents

THE FLESH EATERS 105

MEN AND SAVANNAS 159

APPENDIX

The Savanna Year

East Africa! The very words evoke a vision of broad grassy plains and vast herds of wild animals. Yet as we drive out of Kampala, the modern capital of Uganda near the shores of Lake Victoria, we have the feeling that we might be almost anywhere. The highway is paved, and it is lined with large buildings, gasoline stations, and all the other familiar signs of civilization.

Where, you may wonder, is all the wildlife? It is a good question. At one time great herds of zebras, buffaloes, and various kinds of antelope were abundant almost everywhere in this wild landscape straddling the equator. But Africa is changing rapidly as more and more land is put under cultivation. It is true that in Nairobi, Kenya, it is possible to drive in just a few minutes from the center of the city into the heart of the famous game-filled Nairobi National Park. But elsewhere in Africa the road from the airport to unspoiled countryside nowadays is often rather long. Usually it is necessary to travel twenty, fifty, or even a hundred miles or more to reach an area nearly in its natural state.

Our destination is Murchison Falls National Park in north-western Uganda, nearly two hundred miles away. As we pass beyond the fringes of the city and enter farmlands, we soon begin to notice patches of tall grass and low shrubby trees that look more like what we had expected to see. Suddenly a gray plantain-eater, a large bird with a raucous voice, flies across the road, and we see the gourdlike nests of weaverbirds hanging from trees in villages. Since it is January, the height of the northern tropical dry season, the weavers are not breeding. All the same, they are a tantalizing hint of the varied wildlife we can expect to see at the park.

Fifty miles from the city the paved highway gives way to a dusty gravel road that is badly corrugated by the passage of heavy traffic. Our loaded safari car, equipped with four-wheel drive that will enable it to travel almost anywhere, rattles over the bumps and throws up dense clouds of dust. From time to time we pass hamlets of small grass huts surrounded by fields of sorghum or millet and groves of bananas and coffee trees. Many of the native trees have been destroyed, to be replaced by grass and weeds, but occasionally we pass through stretches of open country that appear to have been little disturbed by man.

With a cloud of dust trailing behind, a safari car bounces along a dirt road across the plains. These rugged vehicles, usually equipped with four-wheel drive, enable the driver to leave the road so that passengers can get an even closer look at the wildlife of the plains.

Eventually as the road grows narrower and bumpier, we pass the last of the small farms and outlying villages and drive into country that seems to be uninhabited. No human beings or cattle are anywhere in sight; a small fly buzzing around inside the car tells us why. It is a tsetse fly, common in many areas of Africa, and it can carry a dreaded disease, *trypanosomiasis,* which affects both men and their livestock. As a result, areas where tsetse flies occur are usually sparsely populated or entirely uninhabited.

The sea of grass

Finally, at midday, we approach a ridge overlooking the edges of Murchison Falls National Park. It is a good time to stop for a rest and have our first real look around before we enter the park itself, for once we are in the park we will not be allowed to get out of the car. This is not because we would be in any danger, but because the animals in the park might begin to associate human beings with cars and be alarmed at the approach of vehicles.

We pull up under a tree and get out, relieved to stretch after the long ride over bumpy roads. Once the rattling and

11

the roar of the engine stop, we begin to notice many new sounds. Barbets, fruit-eating birds that nest in holes in dead tree trunks, are calling in duet nearby. We hear a loud "Keee-ee-ee," and look up to see a long-crested eagle soaring overhead. In the increasing heat of late morning, cicadas shrill in the trees, and we can hear the rattle of dry leaves.

The air is thick with haze, and the leaves on the road are brittle and dry. As we look around we see little more than grass, some of it reaching as high as our heads. Like the leaves, the grass is brown, dry, and lifeless.

To get a better view, we climb a ridge of rock near the roadside. Because of the haze we cannot see far, but everywhere we look the landscape is the same. The gently rolling plains are covered by a sea of tall brown grass, punctuated here and there by gnarled, tough-looking trees that appear completely dead. The trees stand well spaced in the grass, running together on the horizon so that those in the distance look like a low forest. Here at last we are seeing true African *savanna,* as these grass-covered plains with widely scattered trees are generally known.

Savannas of one sort or another cover almost half the surface of Africa—about five million square miles in all—a greater proportion than any other continent. However, vast tracts of wooded savanna (often misnamed forests or simply called jungle) also cover parts of India, Burma, Thailand, and neighboring countries in Asia. In the New World much of interior Brazil and Uruguay is savanna, as are parts of Venezuela and Guyana. The Argentine pampas and the western plains of the United States are temperate grasslands rather than savannas. But the North American prairie, at least in those areas where a natural growth of trees has been curbed by fierce annual fires, is a type of savanna, and there are quite typical savannas in California and Texas. In Australia too, great tracts of grassland studded with low eucalyptus trees or thornless acacias also fit into our broad definition of savannas.

On a typical African savanna, widely spaced umbrella-shaped trees tower above a sea of grass. On clay plains there may be no trees at all, while in semiarid areas the lush grasslands usually give way to dense thickets of thorny brush.

MURCHISON FALLS NATIONAL PARK

Murchison Falls National Park in northwestern Uganda is a mecca that attracts tourists from all over the world. The most famous landmark in the park is the spectacular cascade where the Victoria Nile gushes through a narrow gorge, but the park has other attractions as well. Its 1557 square miles of varied terrain are populated by an incredible wealth of wildlife. Thousands of elephants live here, along with giraffes, rhinos, hippos, lions, leopards, chimpanzees, many kinds of antelope, and an almost unbelievable variety of birds. The most popular tour for viewing this array of animals is on a seven-mile boat trip along the Victoria Nile downstream from the falls. Here, armed only with binoculars and cameras, visitors can easily view and photograph the breathtaking spectacle of African wildlife living in a more or less natural, undisturbed state.

Just below Murchison Falls, a crocodile ambles toward the river (upper). The great number of crocodiles along this section of the Victoria Nile probably is the largest concentration of these magnificent reptiles surviving anywhere in Africa. Hippopotamuses (lower) also are abundant in the river and along its banks, and show little fear of passing boatloads of camera-carrying tourists.

At world famous Murchison Falls (left), the Victoria Nile funnels through a rocky gorge about twenty feet wide and thunders down to a spray-filled abyss. Further downstream the river flows more gently past forested hills on its way to the Nile River proper and then to the Mediterranean Sea some three thousand miles away.

The colorful pygmy kingfisher, one of several species of kingfishers found in Murchison Falls National Park, is only about four inches long, including its inch-long bill. Oddly enough, this kingfisher is likely to be found far from water, for it feeds mainly on insects that it finds in forests and woodlands.

The handsome crowned crane, named for the tuft of bristlelike feathers at the back of its head, sometimes ventures down to the shore of the Victoria Nile in Murchison Falls National Park.

The saddle-bill stork, standing more than four feet high, is one of the tallest of storks. It feeds much as a heron does, standing patiently in shallow water and quickly snatching up unwary fish that venture nearby. Although the saddle-bill is present over a wide range in East Africa, it is seldom seen in great numbers.

Where are all the animals?

As we scan the countryside, we are disappointed at first because we see no lions, giraffes, or herds of zebras. We do see dark rounded humps regularly spaced on open ground among the trees and wonder for a moment if they could be large animals. But they do not move. A closer look through the binoculars reveals that they are not animals at all. They are termite mounds, tall mud structures built by colonies of these industrious, widespread insects.

Although no animals are anywhere in sight, we know from the tracks on the dusty road that they must be somewhere. Then we realize that it is midday and hot; they are probably resting. In any case, the grass is so tall that only the very largest creatures would be visible.

Among the few signs of life are swifts, probably migrants from Europe, flying high in the sky as they hunt for minute insects. Then a bateleur eagle soars over, a magnificent black bird with a short tail and a frosting of silver-white feathers

on the undersides of its very long wings. Of all the birds we shall see, none is more appropriate and familiar in the African savanna than this handsome creature that spends most of its time soaring and travels perhaps two hundred miles daily in search of food.

If we are patient, we will certainly see more animals. Since savannas are found in warm or hot and often moderately moist climates, they form one of the most ideal *habitats*, or living places, for both humans and wild animals. In North America, for example, the plains and prairies once supported great herds of primitive elephants, rhinoceroses, many kinds of bison and deer, and the horses that evolved there. However, most of them had disappeared before the last ice age or even earlier, although a few, such as certain kinds of elephants, horses, and camels, survived long enough in North America to be hunted by men. In Australia, which was separated from the Asian mainland fifty million years ago or more, such great beasts never evolved, and the savannas were populated instead by marsupials, animals such

Where savanna grass stands tall and dry, even a creature as large as a lion can lurk unseen in the tangled growth. Her tawny coat further camouflages this lioness as she peers from a screen of vegetation, possibly scanning the landscape for a potential meal.

as wombats and kangaroos which carry their young in a pouch.

It is only in Africa that the magnificent assembly of wild animals that once populated several of the earth's savannas is still numerous enough for us to study. Even there, although the variety of species is much the same as it was at the beginning of this century, the fossil record indicates a more impressive and luxuriant fauna just a few thousand years ago. Then there were giant baboons, hippopotamuses twice the size of present-day hippos, and wild cattle bigger than any living buffalo.

Now, however, the animals of African savannas have been drastically reduced in numbers, especially within the last thirty years. The magnificent herds that once wandered everywhere have been reduced to remnants living in national parks or in areas where some obstacle, such as the presence of the tsetse fly or shortage of water, prevents exploitation or destructive use by man. Fortunately, however, the remnants that are left are still large and varied enough to enable us to study the animals and how they live.

A closer look at the savanna

At the place where we have stopped at the edge of Murchison Falls National Park in January, it is the height of the dry season, the time when life in the savanna is at its lowest ebb. While tables are being set up in the shade and lunch prepared, we can have a quick look at the vegetation and see what it includes.

A few paces convince us that it consists mainly of grass. With every step we trip over long stems and have to fight our way through the tall dusty growth. Certainly, wherever we go in the African savanna, grass will seldom be out of sight. If we were to cut and weigh the green growing parts of savanna vegetation, we would find that grass outproduces all other forms of plant life. And, as we might expect, most

Weighing in at a ton or more, the black rhinoceros is an impressive reminder of the gigantic, now-extinct creatures that once roamed the African plains. Present-day rhinos are considered "living fossils" since they closely resemble prehistoric ancestors which now are known only through fossil remains.

Like all animals, the wily baboon depends directly or indirectly on living plants for all its food. In addition to eating green grass, it sometimes feasts on insects and small animals that feed in turn on growing plants.

of the animals of the savanna are grass-eaters, or *grazers*. This applies alike to such diverse forms as baboons and buffaloes or to the termites that feed on dead grass. Many of the birds also depend on grass seeds for food.

At the height of the dry season, although seeds and pods are abundant, little green material survives. Most of the trees have dropped their shriveled leaves, and the grass stems, though tall, are hard and tough. If we grip them in passing, they are likely to cut our hands, and anyone who does not wear long trousers is certain to suffer from scratched shins.

Everything seems dead and deserted. Early in the morning or at evening more life would be visible, but at midday few birds move in the trees, and any large animals probably are resting in the shade. The dead grass is so tall that one could hardly see an animal smaller than an elephant anyhow, and the fact that a buffalo or a leopard might be lying still and unseen a few yards away inspires caution as we push through the grass. Later, as we get to know the savanna better, we will realize that the animals are not normally dangerous. But today we keep pausing, perhaps unconsciously searching for a tree to climb if the need should arise.

As we look around we see that the savanna vegetation is

22

made up of three layers. Most obvious of course is the grass layer. Depending on the rainfall in different savanna areas, the grasses may be two to six or even eight feet tall. Most of them are *bunch grasses*—grasses that do not creep to form a solid mat of turf but instead grow in separate well-spaced tufts. Here and there, however, along a small watercourse where a little extra moisture may linger, or on a termite heap where ages of work by the insects have improved both drainage and fertility, we find denser mats of creeping grasses.

Among the grasses there is also an intermediate layer of small shrubs, seldom taller than the grasses themselves, and often lower. Like the grasses, the shrubs seem lifeless, with only a few withered leaves clinging here and there to their wiry stems.

Rising above the grass and shrubs, but seldom more than thirty feet high, is the upper tree layer. Since few of the trees have English names, it is simpler to refer to them by their scientific names. Most common here are acacias, com-

A characteristic tree of dry savannas and arid brushlands, the baobab is sometimes called the upside-down tree—leafless through much of the year, its gnarled branches resemble dry roots projecting from the ground. Like the acacias in moister savannas, baobabs are the tallest plants in their habitat, towering over the intermediate layer of shrubs and the low-lying carpet of grass.

bretums, piliostigmas, terminalias, and erythrinas. The erythrinas are often known as cork trees because of their thick corky bark, and piliostigmas are called camel-foot trees because of the distinctive shape of their leaves.

Like everything else, the leafless trees seem to be dead. If we look more closely, however, we will see that many of the twigs are lined with small buds and are alive right to their tips. Evidently the trees have become dormant in the dry season, just as the trees of temperate woodlands do in winter. In time they will again burst into leaf.

One acacia, which we recognize by its fine feathery leaves and ferocious thorns, already is covered with globular yellow flowers and is humming with bees. Hovering around the blossoms to suck the nectar are several sunbirds. Larger and clumsier than the familiar New World hummingbirds, they are not even closely related to them, but evidently are adapted to live in much the same way as hummingbirds.

Smoke means fire, but fire does not necessarily mean death and destruction. On the savanna, fires ignited by lightning have always been part and parcel of the natural order of things, helping to keep the grasslands free of scrubby vegetation. Today, however, many of the fires are started by men anxious to clear away the dense dry grass.

Death by fire

During lunch a welcome breeze arises, blowing dust and dead leaves about and cooling our perspiring bodies. Suddenly we become aware of a subdued crackling in the distance, and bits of black ash begin to drift down on the table. Behind a line of tall trees along a watercourse, a column of black smoke is rising into the sky, making the haze even thicker and temporarily obscuring the sun. Someone has set the savanna on fire.

The culprit probably was a poacher (one who hunts illegally for game) or a honey hunter trying to make it easier to walk about as he hunts for bees' nests. It is easy enough to understand why they would want to get rid of the tall dense stands of dead grass. Besides being difficult to walk in, there is always the nagging fear of coming upon a leopard or, worse still, a puff adder, a thick-bodied, decora-

tive, but highly venomous snake that is common in savannas. For centuries primitive men, lacking adequate tools, have relied on fire to clear away dead grass. Even today, as the dry season progresses, men set hundreds of fires all over the African savannas.

By the time we reach the source of the smoke, our fire setter has disappeared, but we can see that he started the fire in a bare place at the edge of a rock outcrop. It flickered briefly among partly burned grass stems before taking proper hold and consuming all before it. Probably it was the cooling midday wind that gave it its grip and enabled it to advance with a roar through the tall, tinder-dry grass. Now the flames are leaping fifteen feet high and, at a distance of ten yards, the blast of heat forces us to step back and hold our hands in front of our faces. We wonder how any creature in the grass can survive this scene of total destruction.

Strangely enough, the flames actually provide a feast for

some animals. When the fire started, few birds were moving about in the midday heat. But as the column of smoke thickens and coils into the sky and the roar and crackle of the flames becomes audible from a mile or more away, birds come from all around to feast on the grasshoppers, stick insects, beetles, mice, and lizards that are killed or driven out by the flames. Brilliant carmine bee-eaters and blue rollers perch on dead trees and then swoop almost into the flames to snatch fleeing insects. Hawks, especially black kites and grasshopper buzzards, dive into the smoke to take grasshoppers too big for the smaller birds to eat. Even such unlikely birds as swallows and gray hornbills come to the flames and in a few minutes consume a meal that otherwise would take them hours to find in the dry savanna. When the flames finally die out, great marabou storks and bustards also will come to the burned-over ground and stalk about picking up small dead animals.

With tongues of flame leaping to the sky, a wildfire sweeps through tinder-dry grass on a parched savanna. Although the fire creates a scene of seeming desolation and total destruction, many animals manage to escape the scorching heat.

The survivors

Eventually the flames die down and the fire extinguishes itself. But in its wake, it may leave hundreds or even thousands of acres of scorched earth covered with a fine layer of powdery black ash. Surprisingly, despite the searing heat of the fire itself, which may reach temperatures of 4000 degrees Fahrenheit, it is possible after only a few minutes to step on the burned ground without much discomfort. We search about, hunting for dead mice or snakes that we suppose the fire may have killed. We find very few, however, for most of them are still alive.

At the approach of the flames, some of them took refuge underground in holes and crevices. Although the African plains have nothing comparable to the multitudes of prairie dogs that once flourished throughout American grasslands, there are a few burrowers. In some areas, on well-drained soil, the ground is full of tunnels excavated by mole rats, little molelike rodents that feed on the roots of grasses and trees. Springhares, which are not hares at all but rodents that resemble oversized jerboas, or kangaroo rats, also dig burrows. Their abandoned lairs are often taken over and enlarged by animals such as bat-eared foxes. During a fire, they can provide a safe refuge for all sorts of small creatures.

As for the larger animals, most of them are able to run fast enough to escape a fire, even a fierce one, for the flames,

For some creatures of the savanna, the fire means a time of plenty. At the very fringes of the holocaust, a bustard waits to pounce on small animals fleeing from the flames. Swallows, bee eaters, and other birds dive through the smoke to snatch up grasshoppers and other flying insects.

even when driven by quite a strong wind, travel at little more than a walking pace. The many insects and grubs that were burned or eaten by birds probably did not have long to live in any case. Even so, the devastation caused by the fire seems so complete that it is hard to imagine that anything will be able to live here again for many months.

After the fire

Anxious to see what will happen next, we return to the scene of the fire in March. Now great cumulus clouds pile up in the sky each afternoon and lightning flickers about the horizon at night. Local Africans tell us with relief that the end of the dry season is in sight. Soon the rains will be coming.

All the same, the heat is oppressive as we walk away from the road, and no breath of wind stirs the powdery ash that carpets the ground. Adding to our discomfort are the tiny sweat bees that cluster around our eyes, eager for any drop of moisture. As far as we can see through the thick haze, the land is black and bare, and the midday heat now seems intensified by the constant shrilling of cicadas and the occasional explosive pop of a bursting seed pod.

If we take the temperature of the ground, first in a little patch of unburned grass and then on a bare burned area,

In the wake of the flames, a pair of marabou storks gleans the blackened plain for dead snakes and other creatures killed by the wall of fire. Larger, swifter animals such as the gazelles and zebras on the next two pages are more fortunate; as the fire approaches, they calmly walk away.

we will see the reason for the increased heat we feel. In the grass the temperature is in the nineties or low hundreds, no more than that of the air. But on the bare black earth it is thirty or forty degrees higher—120 to 140 degrees Fahrenheit —and the soil is baked and bricklike.

Although we know large numbers of animals must be present, we see no obvious signs of life. Even the coats of rather brightly colored animals such as the red Jackson's hartebeests are darkened by the ash and dust in which they have rolled, and herds of buffaloes appear only as blacker bulks in a gray landscape. As we stand there, the crack of a breaking branch in a distant thicket reveals the presence of elephants. But we cannot see them.

However, with the grass gone, we feel safer as we walk about. Even puff adders, if above the surface at all, would be more visible on the bare ground than in tall grass. As we progress, we notice that a few tiny blades of green have sprung from each grass tussock. Despite the scorching fire, the grass is still alive. If we were to dig up a tussock, we would see the reason why. We would find that the mass of roots below the ground weighs far more than the dry stems and leaves that stood above the ground, and often penetrates the soil to depths greater than the height the leaves and stems reached in the air. When the rains come, the savanna bunch grasses grow vigorously, producing five to eighteen or more tons of green material per acre. Then, as the dry season comes on, they set seed, and the aboveground parts dry and die back. The mass of roots, with all its starch reserves, remains alive underground, ready to suck up any bit of moisture in the soil and send up new growth.

New shoots have also sprung from the rootstocks of the scattered shrubs. Just as raspberry canes are killed each year by winter cold, the shrubs are killed by the annual fires. Like the raspberries, however, they send up new growth from food reserves in the rootstock when living conditions improve. These first new shoots often are eagerly sought out and eaten by smaller antelope, such as bushbucks and duikers. In fact, they may make the difference between

After the fire has passed, zebras and gazelles return to the plain to graze on the fresh green shoots that spring from the ashes. Although dry stems and leaves were consumed by the flames, the grasses' deep roots remained unharmed and ready to send up new growth.

life and death for these animals, since the dead dry vegetation they fed on before the fire is exceedingly low in the foods they need to remain healthy.

On the trees, too, buds are opening into tender new leaves, and some of them have already burst into flower. Acacias especially are heavy with blossoms, and the erythrinas are covered with clusters of bright-red blooms that attract nectar-feeding sunbirds. In Indian savannas at the same stage of growth, the brilliant orange-flowering dhak tree is frequented by crows, parrots, mynahs, and leaf-bulbuls as well as sunbirds, all in search of nectar. With them is a little striped squirrel that tips up each flower and drinks nectar from it with a comical air of satisfaction.

Unlike the grasses and shrubs, the trees survive the fire by retaining some moisture in all their aboveground parts throughout the dry season. Some of them are sheathed in thick corky bark, while others have semisucculent trunks covered with smooth resinous bark, both of which are more or less fire-resistant. Thus, although their smaller lower branches may be scorched, the upper ones survive and their tips remain full of life even after the fire has passed.

Until the trees are tall enough to have branches that reach beyond the flames, however, their lives are rather difficult. Instead of growing from seeds, many of them start as *suckers,* or shoots growing from underground roots. Indeed, it is often quite difficult to induce the seeds of savanna trees to grow without special treatment. This may involve burning them, rasping them with a file as if they had been ground between the teeth of an animal, or even passing them whole through an animal's digestive tract.

When a young tree finally begins to grow, it may take several years for it to rise above the level of the grass. Some four-foot-tall trees that look like seedlings actually are growing from rootstocks as big as barrels and are probably scores or even hundreds of years old. If three or four years pass without a fire, such a tree will shoot up vigorously and thrust at least some of its branches high enough in the air to escape the worst of the flames when the fires return.

At the end of the savanna's annual dry season, banks of dark, threatening clouds appear in the sky. For Grant's gazelles, however, the dry season means no great hardship since they can survive for long periods without any drinking water.

And then the rains came

Off in the distance a thunderstorm seems to be threatening. We climb a ridge to sit on a rock outcrop at the top and watch the approach of the rain. Here we can see a wide stretch of country, all black and burned. At the edge of the plain, a dark herd of buffaloes rests in the shade of a group of trees in new leaf. The flicking of tails reveals that barely visible waterbucks and hartebeests are also there.

Far away, a flicker of white in the sky betrays the presence of a flock of white storks. Taking advantage of the updrafts on the approaching storm front, they rise to great heights from which, before evening, they will glide many miles northward toward their breeding places in Europe. They are often accompanied by smaller, black and white Abdim's storks, also moving on to breed in savannas north of the equator. There they will be welcomed by country folk as harbingers of rain, just as migrating white storks, swallows, and robins are welcomed in northern lands as harbingers of spring.

By the time we hear thunder, the rain itself is visible—a solid gray wall of water beneath the leaden base of the

cloud. Animals and birds also see the rain. If the storm does not actually pass over them, elephants and antelope will move toward it, apparently aware that in a few days the rain will bring abundant food instead of scarce pickings. Hobbies and kestrels, small falcons that are common on the plains in winter, also move toward the cloud; the rain will bring out swarms of winged termites on which the falcons can gorge before roosting for the night.

There is a feeling of apprehension in the air, like waiting for an explosion. Which indeed it is—a big thundercloud generates more energy than an atom bomb. Before the rain arrives, there is a chill rush of wind, bringing with it the smell of wet earth and raising clouds of dust, yet the air remains oppressive. The buffaloes that were resting in the shade have risen, their backs to the wind, and are moving out to graze.

Then the rain reaches us and strikes. Within a minute the dust that covered the ground is laid down and strong runnels of water swill over the rocks where we sit. We are soaking wet and cold, for the temperature has dropped about thirty degrees, but there is a lightening of the oppression in the air and a sense of relief. We can easily appreciate

The gray veil of an approaching storm drops life-giving moisture on a rolling savanna, now transformed to a lush green pasture by the frequent rains of the tropical wet season. Soon after the storms pass, herds of grazers are attracted by the abundant forage that carpets the slopes and valleys of the plains.

the joy and celebration that accompanies the first rain in almost every African village, for it means that life will begin anew. Crops can be planted, and livestock that were about to starve will begin to fatten and yield milk.

New life reborn

Two weeks later, after several storms, we return in early April and find the savanna completely transformed. Where all had been black and dusty, there is now an unbroken carpet of emerald-green grass, already six inches tall, that grows almost as we watch it. Some of the larger grasses in fact may grow an inch or more in twenty-four hours.

The atmosphere, instead of being hazy with dust and smoke, is clear and sparkling. We can see fifty miles to the hills beyond Lake Albert. The air is cool and pleasant. A fresh breeze blows in the morning, though sometimes it dies down in the afternoon as more life-giving rain clouds pile up in the moist air.

Oblivious of a circling jackal, a zebra licks the damp fur of her newborn foal. The jackal poses no threat to mother or young, however; it is interested only in carrying off the afterbirth, the membranous sac that enveloped the foal before it was born.

The fresh green carpet of grass already provides more than enough food for the few animals that were here before the storms. Others have moved in from surrounding areas where the rains were not so heavy. Sitting on our rocky ridge, we soon make a tally of over a thousand animals in the valley, though it is only a few square miles in extent. Washed by the rain, their coats are bright and clean. The hartebeests and kobs are reddish brown, and the waterbucks, though darker, are still fresh-looking. The buffaloes and elephants on the other hand have been wallowing to their hearts' content in the newly available mud. Instead of their normal black and gray skins, many are stained with bright-red, whitish, or pale-gray mud.

Many of the antelope are accompanied by newborn young. The calves of many savanna antelope are born about the time of these grass rains, as the first storms are called. With so much fresh grass to feed on, their mothers have plenty of milk.

If the rains fail, as they sometimes do, the calves are born anyway. But then they die, for their mothers have no milk and may abandon them. Pregnant females must be able to

A newborn wildebeest calf teeters on rubbery legs as it struggles to its feet. Within hours, the calf will be strong enough to trot along at a steady pace beside the cow as she makes her way across the plain.

39

move swiftly toward good grazing when the rains begin, and the calves must be able to pick themselves up within an hour of birth and run with their dams. If they are too weak to follow, many of them die or are killed by other animals.

The rebirth of the savanna is far more dramatic than the gradual unfolding of spring in temperate climates. On the burned savanna, one week there is almost nothing to eat and the next there is superabundant green life. Nor does this affect only the grass-eaters. Where before no birds sang at midday, many now advertise their presence with song. Flappet larks and grass warblers rise into the sky on rapidly beating wings, producing a burring sound almost like that of a chain saw. Brilliant blue and brown rollers screech raucously as they hurl themselves about the sky in nuptial acrobatics. Guinea fowl, which had gathered into huge flocks during the dry season, have now separated into pairs that run about madly in the short grass. Before long they will nest and begin to lay eggs.

Close to a stream, where a branch overhangs a pool, yellow weaverbirds already have built their nests, using either grass or strips torn from palm leaves. One species, the red-headed weaver, makes an ingenious nest of twigs, tearing from each one a little strip of bark with which it ties the twig to others in the nest. The result, so sturdy that it may last for years, looks like a downward-pointing flask of loosely woven meshwork.

During the dry season, weaverbirds are often dull and sparrowlike, but just before the rains come they molt into bright breeding colors. Especially striking are the red and black bishop birds and the long-tailed whydahs, or widow birds, in black and yellow. At this time of year the Hausa people of northern Nigeria have a saying which means, "See, the king has put on his robe." They are referring to the orange-red and black bishop bird, which is as brilliant as a ball of fire. When they see the birds' plumage change from dull sparrowy hues to bright red, the people know the rains are not far away.

Ruffled feathers almost double the size of a red bishop bird as it displays before its nest. Like other weaverbirds, the red bishop constructs a neatly woven globular nest of vegetation with an entrance hole opening to a snug chamber inside.

Tail included, the red-collared
widow bird is nearly a foot
long. Even more impressive is
the long-tailed widow bird, with
a train of tail feathers over two
feet long.

Dangling upside down at the entrance
to its nest, a male spotted-backed
weaverbird (*upper*) quivers its wings
in a display designed to attract a female
to the nest. In the lower picture, a tree
is decorated with the hanging nests of
a colonial species of weaverbird.

A loosely bound framework of twigs defines the outline of the uncompleted nest of a redheaded weaverbird. Although most weavers use flexible bits of vegetation such as grass, this species prefers to build with twigs and other coarse material.

Chimneylike towers of a termite mound (*right*) rise like strange sculpture from an African plain. Below, winged adult termites, surrounded by wingless individuals, emerge from crevices in the mound. Sometimes swarms of a million or more winged adults emerge from a single colony.

The universal provider

Part of the reason for the burst of new life among birds is the sudden abundance of insects. At night it becomes unpleasant to sit near a campfire because of the myriads of large black scarab beetles that are attracted by the light.

The most spectacular insect flights are provided by the swarms of winged termites that now leave their underground nests to form new colonies elsewhere. Early in the rainy season great clouds of them emerge each evening from holes in the ground and rise in feeble flight. Most of them are seized by insect-eating birds such as flycatchers, swallows, rollers, and nightjars. Even large eagles stand beside the holes and gobble up the emerging insects. Nor do men disdain the flying termite which is full of fat and, when fried, tastes like crisp bacon rind. Some African people actually tap the mounds with sticks to simulate the patter of raindrops, thus inducing the flying individuals to emerge.

Despite all these hazards, some of the termites manage to escape and establish colonies. The winged males and females never fly far—a few hundred yards at most. Of the million or more individuals that may emerge from a mound in a single night, a few land and immediately drop their wings. Once they are wingless and back on the ground, several

44

males follow a single female, and one eventually pairs with her. The two then seek a safe place, such as under a stone, and build a nest chamber. When this is complete, they mate and the female begins to lay eggs.

Over the years, the colony continues to grow and flourish until it includes millions of individual termites. The workers gradually build up a large mound of hardened clay whose form varies, depending on the species of termite that builds it. In East African savannas the most common type is a rounded hump twenty to thirty feet across and up to six or seven feet high, with many vertical shafts letting air into the mound.

Eventually, however, the colony begins to weaken as fewer and fewer new individuals are produced. Finally it dies out, perhaps thirty years after it was originally founded. Even then the mounds, dotted evenly over the landscape, remain for many years as monuments to the termites' activities.

Since the mounds are composed of mixtures of saliva and soil carried up from a depth, and are shot through and through with tunnels, they are both more fertile and better drained than the surrounding land. As a result, different, sweeter kinds of grass grow on them. During the dry season these grasses are eagerly sought by grazing animals in need

Elephants sometimes use termite mounds for scratching posts. As the great beasts rub against the mounds, they gradually grind them down, returning the fertile, hard-packed mortar to the soil.

45

Even when termite mounds have worn down to little more than humps on the plain, they continue to serve the needs of other animals. Here an old mound provides a lookout post for a male Peter's gazelle, a variety of Grant's gazelle which is found in a few arid areas of northern Kenya.

of nutritious forage. In addition, one type of savanna common in southwestern Kenya, Tanzania, and Uganda, known as grouped-tree grassland, has trees growing only on termite mounds—the intervening soil is too shallow or too poorly drained to support the growth of any trees at all.

The mounds fill other needs as well. Hartebeests and other antelope use them as lookout posts and central points in their territories. Lions climb upon them to spot potential prey in the distance. And in Murchison Falls National Park, elephants scratch themselves on the mounds, probably because they have recently killed all the good scratching trees. Eventually the elephants completely demolish the mounds, and thus return the concentrated nutrients to the soil.

However, the termites' main contribution to the savanna community is as a source of food. One notable termite-eater is a unique animal, the aardvaark, or antbear. Using its powerful forefeet and claws, the aardvaark easily digs holes into bricklike termite mounds. It then pushes its long snout and sticky tongue into exposed tunnels to lick up the insects. It does not exterminate the termites in any colony, however, but harvests them from several mounds in regular rotation.

All sorts of insectivorous birds also feast on termites, especially in the dry season, as do a number of small mammals such as mongooses and the ungainly aardwolf. While this feeding on surplus termites is continuous, however, it does not exterminate the sightless, slow-moving insects. They are always abundant and continually breaking down and digesting plant matter, which they convert into their own living tissue. This in turn serves as food for myriad other creatures who would often be hard put to survive without these universal providers.

What the grasses tell us

By May, the appearance of the savanna has changed again. Everywhere we look it is carpeted with rich varied shades of green; hardly any bare earth is visible. With warm air and plenty of moisture, the surge of new growth rushes on unabated. Just a month after the rains began, some of the

Cheetahs also favor termite mounds, both as lookout posts where they can scan the plains for potential prey and as comfortable resting places where they can simply loll in the sun.

earliest grasses already are throwing up their first seedheads. Now is the time to walk through the savanna and appreciate the wonderful variety of form and function of the grasses.

Because the savanna supports such a tremendous number of different species competing for living space, it usually happens that one or a few kinds of grass are more successful than all others in a particular area. They push out or dwarf all the rest. Thus stretches of savanna come to be dominated by from one or two to half a dozen species that are especially well adapted for life on a particular soil type. These are called *dominants.*

On the foothills above Murchison Falls National Park, for example, the dominant tall grasses are various species of hood grasses and guinea grasses. Two species of these grasses, in fact, are so adaptable that they have colonized other continents and become *pantropical*, which means that they occur everywhere in the tropics.

Down on the valley floor, in contrast, the soil is more clayey and there is more moisture. Here we find that the

savanna is dominated by bristle grasses. Still other species flourish where the soil is boggy around a pool. Near streams, where there is no forest, very tall varieties of guinea grass, wild sugar canes, and wild sorghums prevail. Each kind of grass, in other words, can become dominant under a particular set of living conditions.

With experience, it is possible to travel to African savannas hundreds of miles apart and, by looking at the dominant grasses, make a fairly accurate estimate of the average annual rainfall in each locality. Different kinds of grasses, moreover, grow on red or black soils. Thus by sitting on a rock or termite mound and noticing patches of different kinds of grass in head, we can make a rough kind of mental soil map of the area. This kind of specific adaptation to particular situations is also true of trees. By examining an aerial photograph through a stereoscope, an expert can identify the dominant trees. Knowing this, he can then predict what kinds of crops and livestock would probably thrive in the area without actually visiting it.

Kopjes, small hills of piled granite boulders like this one on the Serengeti plains of Tanzania, are a common sight on African savannas. From such a vantage point, it is possible to distinguish patches of different kinds of grass on the surrounding plain, each kind growing under slightly different soil conditions.

The variety of growing grasses

In drier savannas such as those on the Serengeti plains or on Kenya's Laikipia plateau, the dominants on well-drained soils are Rhodes grass and red oat grass. Both of them flourish in climates where hood grasses tend to become small and weak.

Throughout the East African savannas some of the most valuable grasses are star grasses. Since they like fertile spots, they often grow on termite mounds in the middle of plains dominated by red oat grass. They also spring up where cattle regularly congregate. Old Masai villages, or *manyattas*, even half a century after they have been abandoned, are usually marked by dark-green patches of star grass that are visible at once from an airplane or hilltop.

Most of these grasses are palatable, at least when young, and many cure readily to make good standing hay. Some of the grasses, however, are actually unpalatable or so stiff and wiry as to be almost inedible. The lemon grasses, for example, which are common in many western Uganda savannas, contain a sweet-scented but very bitter oil in their leaves. No animal will eat them, except when the grasses are young, unless it can find nothing else.

The wire grasses, in contrast, are not so much unpalatable as physically inedible. Their stems are stiff and wirelike and are ringed with whorls of spiky leaves. Zebras and donkeys, which have cutting teeth in both jaws, can manage to eat some dry wire grass. But cattle will starve if no other grasses are available since they have cutting teeth only in their lower jaws and are unable to bite the wiry stems.

End and beginning

The rainy season often ends as it began, with a series of violent thunderstorms. Finally, one day in October we wake to clear skies, and a strong drying wind blows, telling us that the long dry season has begun. In the Guinea savanna of West Africa, the wind comes from the north or northeast, bringing with it fine dust from the Sahara and making the atmosphere so hazy that visibility is reduced to a mile or less. In southern savannas the onset of the dry season is often sudden enough to produce autumnal tints in the dying leaves

Two widespread grasses on African savannas are star grass (*below*) and the much taller red oat grass (*opposite*). Both are nutritious and provide good fodder for grazing animals. Like many grasses, red oat grass spreads not only by seeds, but also by means of rhizomes, underground stems that produce new shoots. Star grass produces stolons, stems that grow along the surface of the ground and send up new shoots here and there along their length. Like red oat grass, it also produces rhizomes.

similar to those one sees in forests in temperate regions. Most of the trees take on various shades of gold and yellow, but a few, such as the incense tree, turn bright red, almost like a maple.

The grass by now is often taller than a man's head, and the stems and leaves are no longer tender; they have hardened and become more fibrous. Worse still, they are less nutritious. On the average, grass-eating savanna animals require about six or seven percent protein in their diets. When the grass is young and plentiful, it contains more than enough protein to meet this need, but in the dry season the protein content of the grass may be only two percent. Thus, as the rain fails and the grass dries up, the leaves and fruits of trees and the remaining green tips of shrubs become more important as sources of protein. The fruits of fig trees, which are common along streams, for example, are eaten avidly by all sorts of fruit-eating birds, by monkeys and baboons, and, when they have fallen to the ground, by elephants, wild hogs, and certain antelope.

By now human beings are busy harvesting their crops, and for them it is a time of plenty, feasting, and play. But for their livestock and for wild animals, the time of privation and difficulty is near at hand. A month ago they could still get a meal of fairly nourishing food with little difficulty; now they can find it only by picking selectively at the more nutritious portions of plants.

While much of the vegetation is useless, however, most of the animals will face the approaching time of hardship with a good chance of survival. Cattle may lose as much as a third of their weight in the next four months, but now, early in the dry season, most of them are sleek and fat and their young usually have been weaned from their mothers' milk.

Are the fires fatal?

We are now back almost where we started, stepping off the road into a tangle of tall dead grass. Soon it will be so dry that the slightest spark could set off a roaring blaze. But by following the savanna year through its full cycle, we know now that the fire is not likely to kill the grass.

In fact, if fires were stopped altogether, as many would advise, the grass would not necessarily benefit. Experiments

Fighting their way up through a vigorously growing cover of grass, shrubby young acacias gradually gain a foothold in an area that had once been swept by fire. Eventually some of them probably will grow tall enough to survive even if the area is burned again.

have shown that grass entirely protected from fire and not shaded by trees eventually grows weak and dies out, to be replaced by other less vigorous species. Some grasses, such as the common red oat grass, actually thrive better if frequently burned.

Moreover, if a tract of savanna is totally protected from fire for ten years or so, the shrubs and trees are likely to shoot up and gradually shade out the grass. Heavy grazing on tall grass by cattle and wild animals also encourages the growth of trees and shrubs and eventually results in thickets and woodlands where once—perhaps only a generation or so ago—there was open savanna.

On the other hand, a heavy concentration of animals such as elephants, which feed on leaves and twigs, can convert quite a dense woodland into open grassland in a surprisingly short time. Once they have destroyed the trees, annual fires will maintain the area as savanna.

52

The elephant problem

This is precisely what is happening in some areas. Late in the nineteenth and early in the twentieth century, elephants in many parts of Africa were practically exterminated by hunters who killed them for the sake of their ivory tusks. Eventually the colonial governments prohibited this slaughter, and the herds again increased in number. But so did human beings, and more and more people moved into formerly uninhabited areas. If the elephants tried to remain, they were either chased away by the newcomers or, because they ate crops, were shot by game wardens. Thus they tended to move away into the steadily shrinking tracts of uninhabited country. Even here a certain amount of licensed hunting still discouraged them. Finally they could find complete protection only in national parks or in areas where no shooting was permitted, and there the elephants are creating a real problem.

The difficulty arises from the fact that elephants not only eat, but also smash, the vegetation, much as a bulldozer does. Besides breaking off small branches, they use their foreheads to push against and uproot fairly large trees. They kill even bigger trees by girdling them—they dig at the bark with their tusks and, when a strip has been loosened, seize it with their trunks and pull. In time all the bark is stripped away and the tree dies. Even baobab trees, which have semisucculent fibrous trunks without true wood, are easily torn to pieces by elephants—a feat that even the largest bulldozers cannot match!

At one time much of Murchison Falls National Park was covered with mixed savanna of tall grasses and quite dense woodlands. Now, because there are so many elephants, hardly a tree has been left standing in many areas. Yet the elephants cannot leave the park and seek trees elsewhere, because outside the park there are too many people. Instead they feed on the tall grasses which flourish now that the trees are gone. This same sort of thing is happening in every African national park where elephants are numerous, all the way from the Union of South Africa to Kenya and Uganda.

The only way to solve the elephant problem and end this massive destruction of habitat is to reduce the number of elephants. Yet few people care to think of elephants being

Elephants are capable of badly damaging and even killing large trees. They strip off bark and break branches with their trunks and sometimes push the trees over with their massive foreheads. In many parks where elephants are abundant, they are drastically changing the landscape by destroying most of the trees.

shot by the thousands. Moreover, unless such wholesale slaughter were carried out by eliminating entire family groups, babies and all, the survivors would become so shy that they would not permit tourists to approach them and enjoy the magnificent spectacle of their existence.

In any case, in Murchison Falls National Park it is unlikely that even massive shooting campaigns would result in renewed growth of trees. This is an area where fires in the dry season are fierce, and as long as they continue, young trees will not be able to grow even if all the elephants are removed.

One hopeful sign is the fact that, now that grass is so abundant in the park, buffaloes are becoming more numerous. Eventually there may be enough of them to suppress the growth of long grasses and help reduce the frequency and severity of fires. But it will be many years before that happens. In the meantime, the trees are gone, and so are

Like members of a circus parade, a herd of elephants marches across the plains in Murchison Falls National Park, where the huge beasts are so numerous that they have practically eliminated the trees in many areas.

many of the birds and mammals that characterized the park at the beginning of the century.

The only alternative is to wait for the elephants to decline in numbers through natural causes. To some extent this already seems to be happening at Murchison Falls National Park. The elephants are maturing later than normal and producing fewer calves than in other areas. But here and in other parks with an elephant problem, the controversy continues as to whether their numbers should be controlled by killing some of the excess. Even if the population eventually decreases of its own accord, it will take several decades before we can be certain that this is actually happening since elephants live so long. By then they will have altered the habitat for better or worse—and perhaps irrevocably. The vegetation in many of the parks already is far different from what it was only twenty or thirty years ago. In the life of a savanna, that is a very short time indeed.

What makes a savanna?

Since so much of the earth's surface, especially in Africa, is covered with savanna of one sort or another, it is worth considering the conditions that create this type of vegetation. The first and most important factor is climate. Savannas are always found in warm or hot climates where the annual rainfall is from about twenty to fifty inches per year. The most typical forms occur in tropical areas with an annual rainfall of thirty to forty inches.

The crucial factor, however, is that the rainfall must be concentrated in six or eight months of the year, followed by a long period of drought when fires can occur. If the rain were well distributed throughout the year, many such areas would be covered by tropical forest instead of a mixture of grass and drought-resistant trees. Savannas of this sort, which result from these special climatic conditions, are known as true *climatic savannas.*

But there are other types of savanna as well. In high rainfall areas such as occur in Nigeria, Uganda, and the Congo, patches of savanna often exist in densely forested country. A traveler in such an area may find himself walking one moment in cool dark forest and the next in blazing sunlight on open grassland.

Such a great difference within a hundred yards obviously cannot result from climatic variation. As it happens, these patches of savanna are often found at the bases and summits of hills or ridges. They also occur in broad flat valleys such as the llanos of the Orinoco River and the flood plain of the Niger River. Their principal cause is soil conditions. Those found on hills or ridges are growing where the soil is too shallow and the underlying rocks are too close to the surface to permit the growth of big forest trees. Those found in valleys are growing in clay soils that become waterlogged in wet weather, conditions that do not favor the growth of forests.

Such savannas are known as *edaphic savannas* since they are associated with certain soil types and are not entirely maintained by fire. Even if fires are stopped, they will not become forest. Their existence is important, for it helps to prove that patches of savanna existed before man appeared on the scene and learned to use fire.

A third type of savanna, known as *derived savanna*, is made by men as they clear forest land for cultivation. Most

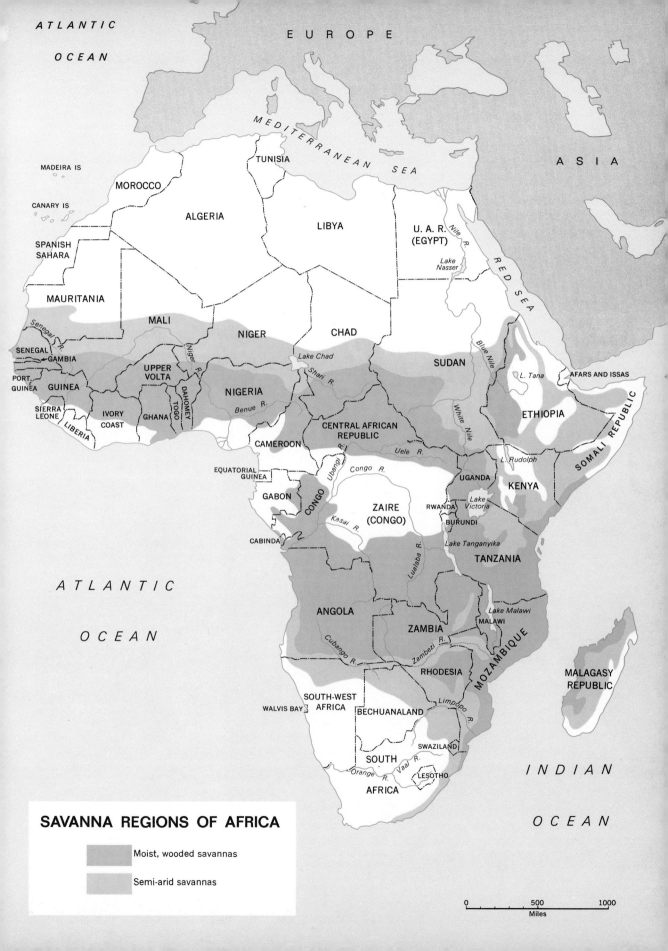

ATLANTIC
OCEAN

EUROPE

ASIA

MEDITERRANEAN SEA

MADEIRA IS

MOROCCO

TUNISIA

CANARY IS

SPANISH
SAHARA

ALGERIA

LIBYA

U. A. R.
(EGYPT)

Nile R.

Lake
Nasser

RED SEA

MAURITANIA

Senegal R.

MALI

NIGER

CHAD

SENEGAL
GAMBIA

PORT.
GUINEA   GUINEA

UPPER
VOLTA

Niger R.

Lake Chad

Shari R.

SUDAN

Blue Nile

L. Tana

AFARS AND ISSAS

SIERRA
LEONE

IVORY
COAST

LIBERIA

GHANA

DAHOMEY
TOGO

NIGERIA

Benue R.

CAMEROON

CENTRAL AFRICAN
REPUBLIC

Uele R.

White Nile

ETHIOPIA

SOMALI REPUBLIC

EQUATORIAL
GUINEA

GABON

CONGO

Ubangi R.

Congo R.

ZAIRE
(CONGO)

Kasai R.

UGANDA

RWANDA

Lake
Victoria

KENYA

L. Rudolph

CABINDA

BURUNDI

Lualaba R.

Lake Tanganyika

TANZANIA

ATLANTIC

OCEAN

ANGOLA

Cubango R.

ZAMBIA

Zambezi R.

Lake Malawi

MALAWI

MOZAMBIQUE

MALAGASY
REPUBLIC

SOUTH-WEST
AFRICA

WALVIS BAY

BECHUANALAND

RHODESIA

Limpopo R.

INDIAN

SWAZILAND

SOUTH

Orange R.

Vaal R.

LESOTHO

AFRICA

OCEAN

SAVANNA REGIONS OF AFRICA

Moist, wooded savannas

Semi-arid savannas

0   500   1000
Miles

country people in Africa, Asia, and tropical America practice what is called *shifting cultivation*. They fell a tract of forest, burn the dead trees, and plant crops in the ashes for as long as any fertility remains in the soil. Then after a few years they abandon the field and clear another patch of land elsewhere. Although forest trees may recolonize the abandoned field, grass often takes over on the bare ground, becoming luxuriant enough to burn within a year or so.

Of these three types of savanna, the first, true climatic savanna, is produced by the immutable oscillation of the earth on its axis, which results in the passage of the sun north and south across the equator and, at certain latitudes, produces a climate with a long dry season. The second type, edaphic savanna, results from long, continued processes of erosion that may have been accelerated by man within the last thousand years or so, but began long before man appeared on the scene. The third, derived savanna, which is rapidly spreading in all tropical lands and eating into the reserves of forest, is caused by man.

Many authorities believe that all African savannas must have been created by man and his use of fire. They feel that if we could stop the fires, all land now covered by savanna would gradually become forested or at least heavily wooded. Yet natural fires must have burned savannas from time to time even before man learned to make extensive use of fire. And certain tracts, especially edaphic savannas, would persist even if they were never burned. In these at least, some of the savanna animals must have survived long before man appeared on the earth.

So we can conclude that most savanna in Africa probably is an old form of vegetation, in which the varied savanna animals we know today were able to evolve. Man by his frequent use of fire certainly has modified and extended the savanna. But he probably did not create it.

In a spot charred by a recent fire, tender new shoots sprout from the undamaged roots of a savanna shrub. Subjected to repeated burnings over thousands of years, the plants of the savanna have evolved means for surviving the fires that periodically sweep across the plains.

Productive
Pastures

South of Kenya, in Tanzania, is Serengeti National Park, one of the most famous wild animal sanctuaries in the world. The park, five thousand square miles in extent, lies just south of the Kenya-Tanzania border and east of Lake Victoria. It is an exceptionally fine place to take a closer look at the vast herds of wild animals whose lives depend on the natural pastures of the savanna.

For one thing, Serengeti includes a number of different savanna habitats, each with somewhat different animal populations. The area around Seronera, the park head-quarters located near the center of the reserve, is surrounded by acacia woodlands. The dark-green, flat-topped trees stand well spaced in a carpet of tall red oat grass, creating a scene very much like the usual notion of a typical African landscape. In every patch of shade we expect to see groups of lions or herds of zebras or hartebeests. Yet within a few miles one can travel to entirely different landscapes. Both long-grass savanna and open short-grass plains are nearby.

The greatest wildlife attraction at Serengeti is the annual migration of animals across the park. When the rains start,

often in November, herds of wildebeests, zebras, and gazelles travel south across the park to the open short-grass plains. Then in June, at the end of the rainy season, they travel west to the wooded long-grass savanna. By August and September they are on the move again, to the north of the park, completing their more or less triangular route.

When the herds are on the move, they provide the greatest spectacle of its kind left on earth. As they pass through, the area around Seronera for a few weeks holds so many animals that it is difficult to sleep at night because of their continual grunting and braying and the pounding of their hooves on hard ground.

The grazing multitude

If we drive southeast from Seronera in January, we emerge in a few miles on completely open short-grass plains. Here and there the plains are studded with small hills of granite boulders, known as *kopjes*. We climb one, for it is a good lookout point from which to spy over the plains for the great herds we seek. The grass is green after recent rains, the air is sparkling and clear, and a fresh breeze blows. Although we are very close to the equator, we are over five thousand feet above sea level, so it is quite comfortable to sit out in the open without any shelter from the sun.

Dotted at intervals over the plain are many small herds of yellow-brown Thomson's gazelles. Those in the distance are difficult to see except when they turn their white buttocks toward us as they feed. Farther off we see a blackish bulk perched on a termite mound. A closer look reveals that it is a topi bull standing there like a sentinel, apparently scanning the landscape for signs of danger.

Still farther away, at the crest of the next gently swelling ridge, the green landscape seems to darken and writhe with movement. And there they are—hundreds of thousands of zebras and wildebeests. The nearer animals are individually distinguishable, but even when we look through binoculars,

The wildebeests in Tanzania's Serengeti National Park periodically migrate across the plains in herds that number in the tens of thousands. Traveling along well-defined routes, they complete a more or less triangular circuit over the course of the year.

the further ones appear to coalesce into one huge mass that stretches as far as the eye can see. Their bodies seem so densely packed that they hide every bit of ground and obscure the smaller, more colorful Thomson's gazelles that wander among the herds.

To get a better look we climb back into the car and drive over toward the herd. It is easy to drive across the plain, for all the grass has been mowed down by the teeth of countless grazers. Provided we keep a sharp lookout for holes, we can maintain a steady speed of twenty miles an hour.

Soon we are among the wildebeest and zebra. Driving into what seems to be a densely packed throng, we find that the animals are actually well spread out over a vast area. We could, in fact, drive for five miles in a straight line without reaching the far side of the living mass. The passage of our car has only a momentary effect on the animals. Those in front of us move away a few yards and continue their grazing, while in a few seconds others move in to fill the temporarily empty space behind us. When we stop, we are so completely surrounded that we can see no part of the real horizon of the plains. All we see are the black moving backs of thousands of animals.

Once the engine falls silent, we become aware of the continuous background of sound—short, deep, lowing grunts; the bleating of calves; the steady pounding of hooves; and a strange hissing whisper of green grass continually being cropped.

Seen from close range, the wildebeests in the Serengeti appear as a solid wall of living animals. The vast herds in the park—estimated to include about 750,000 animals—require enormous tracts of grazing lands if they are to thrive.

Most of the animals are wildebeests, also called brindled gnus. They are blackish, ungainly, bearded antelope, two-thirds the size of a cow, with grotesque heads and sloping backs. The females are accompanied by small calves, brownish and hornless, but already able to run as fast as their parents when it is necessary to escape from a predator. Last year's calves, a little more than a year old, are here too. They are nearly as tall as the adults, but their horns are short and spiky instead of curved like the adults'. Groups of bulls stand apart from the herds of cows and calves, and as we approach they leap away, beards flowing on the wind and tails lashing.

Normally few other animals mingle with the huge throngs of wildebeests. But if we travel to other parts of the same plain, we will come upon herds of thousands of zebras, which trot away in small groups as we approach. Elsewhere there are scores of herds of Thomson's gazelles and groups of the larger, long-horned Grant's gazelles. The Grant's gazelles are the chief permanent residents of the plains. They will remain here when, after a stay of about five months, the wildebeests, zebras, and smaller gazelles have migrated to the long-grass savannas.

Here and there we also find a few herds of fifty to one hundred elands. The elands are among the largest of the living antelope, and their heads are surmounted by angled, spearlike horns. Unlike the wildebeests, they are always shy and will not allow a close approach. Small herds of topis also roam the plains, and now and then we spot a hyena or

The most numerous of all grazers on the Serengeti plains are Thomson's gazelles, with a population of over one million individuals. These graceful little antelope are only about two feet high at the shoulder and weigh about forty pounds.

a jackal, mud-stained from life in a damp burrow or in the case of hyenas, from bathing in muddy pools. Even when hyenas lie out in the open, they cause very little excitement among the moving throng of grazers; as long as the hyenas are clearly visible, they seem to be regarded as harmless.

How many animals?

Seeing wild animals in such vast numbers, all of them apparently sleek and healthy, we can see that savannas are truly productive pastures. It is easy to understand, too, how the first people to look upon such throngs of *herbivores*, or plant-eaters, could have believed that they could keep just as many cattle and sheep on the same ground. Yet, as we shall see, in many places where domestic livestock has been brought in, the pasture is almost always poorer and less productive as a result.

As we return from our day on the plains, we may feel inclined to try to guess exactly how many animals we have seen. Even a small part of the herds of wildebeests and zebras that we have passed is hard to count directly, however. When we look at the animals from a little farther away, continually shifting and disappearing behind others, we give up in despair. Individual herds of gazelles scattered over the landscape are easier to count, but even there we find that new groups keep appearing from low spots between the ridges or from behind bushes.

Fortunately, however, the migrations are observed each year by scientists from the Serengeti Research Institute, the foremost among several wildlife research stations based in East Africa. Using a variety of modern techniques, including computers, they have come up with quite accurate estimates of the number of animals in the park. Some species, such as rhinoceroses, which haunt thick brush are very difficult to count accurately. Others, especially the large blackish

Standing three feet tall at the shoulder and weighing up to 175 pounds, Grant's gazelles are crowned by horns that sometimes are as much as thirty inches long. These two are accompanied by a cattle egret, waiting to snatch insects stirred up by the gazelles' hooves.

1 ELEPHANT (10,000 POUNDS)

4 BLACK RHINOS (2500 POUNDS EACH)

15½ ZEBRAS (650 POUNDS EACH)

27 HARTEBEESTS (370 POUNDS EACH)

As a measure of the productivity of an area, the standing crop biomass, or total weight of animals living there, is more meaningful than mere numbers. This is so because animals vary so much in size. A single 10,000-pound elephant, for example, weighs about the same as fifteen and a half 650-pound zebras or twenty-seven 370-pound hartebeests. In contrast, it takes two hundred fifty 40-pound Thomson's gazelles to equal the weight of a 5-ton elephant.

species such as buffaloes and elephants, which stand out clearly on the landscape, are quite easy to count directly. For the huge, continually moving mixed herds on the plains, however, more sophisticated techniques such as aerial surveys must be employed.

Using all these methods, the scientists have come up with some astonishing totals, especially for the migrating herds. From their work we know that, since 1961, the wildebeests have increased in number each year so that now there are nearly twice as many as there were a decade ago. The total number in Serengeti is about 750,000. In addition, there are over 1 million Thomson's gazelles and probably around 200,000 zebras, though these have been less accurately estimated than the others. The grand total of these migrants alone, then, is nearly 2 million individual animals!

Standing crop biomass

The scientists have taken their calculations a step further, however. What they would really like to know is the actual total weight of live animals that can be supported throughout the year in a given area, a statistic known as the *standing crop biomass*. This can be calculated by multiplying the number of animals by their average weights. Knowing that a Thomson's gazelle, on the average, weighs about 40 pounds, a wildebeest about 350 pounds, and a zebra about 650 pounds, we come up with a total standing crop biomass for these migrants of slightly more than 430 million pounds. Since the whole area over which the animals wander is about 8000 square miles, we can say that the standing crop biomass for these species alone is about 54,000 pounds per square mile.

The point of all these calculations is to enable us to compare the efficiency of wild and domestic animals in using the grassland. Throughout the world, ranchers estimate the *carrying capacity* of their land (the maximum number of a particular kind of animal that can be supported year-round per unit of habitat) in terms of *standard livestock units*. A standard livestock unit is simply a handy label meaning 1,000 pounds of living animal. Thus, one cow with a small calf is considered to be a standard livestock unit, as are five adult European sheep, which weigh about 200

68

pounds each. In Africa, however, native cattle and sheep are generally stunted from poor feeding and bad management. A cow may weigh only 500 pounds and sheep only 40 to 50 pounds. Here we can say that two cows or at least twenty sheep are required to make up a standard unit.

By pulling together all the figures for all the animals at Serengeti, the scientists have concluded that the overall biomass of the area comes to something like one livestock unit per eight acres. This is far greater than the weight of domestic animals that any rancher could keep in the same area. Even the most optimistic stockman would never expect to keep two cows or twenty sheep on eight acres of the Serengeti throughout the year.

In some savannas, the biomass is even greater than at Serengeti. The highest ever recorded is for Queen Elizabeth National Park in Uganda, with a total biomass of about 250,000 pounds per square mile, or one livestock unit per two and a half acres, about as good as a first-class dairy pasture in a temperate climate. Several other savannas exceed 100,000 pounds per square mile of wild animals.

A sequence of grazers

How then can so many wild animals manage to survive in the Serengeti? Their migrations of course tell part of the story. By moving from place to place with the changing seasons, they do not overuse and damage the grass in any one area. But other less obvious factors also are involved.

Here on the eastern plains in January, it is clear that most of the animals are eating the abundant grass that springs up like a well-mown lawn between low clumps of Sodom apple and indigo plants. Nearly all of them, from 1,500-pound eland bulls to tiny 10-pound Thomson's gazelle calves, are grazers, rather than *browsers*, which feed on shrubs or the leaves of trees. Singly or in pairs, long lines, or little groups, they move over the green pastures, never remaining long in one place. Where the grass is all short, as it will be when it has been heavily grazed, all the animals apparently eat much the same sort of grass. But where the grass is of varied lengths and toughness, we can see that each animal copes differently with the available fodder.

The herds of zebras, as we have seen, tend to roam in areas

ONE STANDARD LIVESTOCK UNIT

1 COW AND SMALL CALF (1000 POUNDS)

2 AFRICAN COWS (500 POUNDS EACH)

5 EUROPEAN SHEEP (200 POUNDS EACH)

20 AFRICAN SHEEP (50 POUNDS EACH)

Ranchers frequently measure the number of animals an area can support in terms of standard livestock units, with one livestock unit equalling 1000 pounds of living animal. Thus one livestock unit can include one healthy cow with a small calf or five 200-pound sheep. In Africa, however, where domestic animals are often stunted as a result of poor management, relatively greater numbers of smaller animals are required to make up one standard livestock unit.

separate from the rest of the grazing multitude. Unlike all the other grazers on the plain, they have teeth in both jaws. This enables them to deal with taller, coarser grass than can the other herbivores. All the rest are various species of antelope, which nip off the grass between their lower incisors and toothless upper palates. Thus the zebras eat down the longer grasses to a certain level and then move on.

Following the zebras come the wildebeests and, in better wooded areas, hartebeests. These animals eat the grass down a stage further, until it is really short. (They also eat new growth before it has had a chance to grow tall.) Then the Thomson's gazelles take over. With their tails flickering constantly, they nibble at the individual leaves of the tussocks and on the tiny plants that grow between them. By the time all of them have finished, the plain resembles a closely but rather unevenly mown lawn.

Thus, one species or another of animal often predominates over a great expanse of the plain, depending on the height to which the grass has grown or been grazed. Finally, when all has been eaten down rather short, most of the grazers leave the area altogether.

Two or three weeks later, when more rain has brought on fresh growth, the herds may return to feed over the area again. Perhaps they move about in response to the intensity of local showers, which can vary a good deal over a distance of only a mile or two. In any case, the result of their returning again and again to the same areas is to keep the grass green and short, just as the repeated mowing of a lawn in summer does.

If, as a result of badly drawn park boundaries or some other cause, the migrant herds of Serengeti were confined to either the western woodlands or the eastern short-grass plains, they would be forced to return to the same areas too often and would eventually so weaken the grass that it would die out. But as they eat it down, they move away and the grass recovers.

The rare Grevy's zebra, a resident of northern Kenya, Ethiopia, and Somalia, is easily distinguished from the commoner, more widely distributed Burchell's zebra by its much narrower, more numerous stripes. Like the Burchell's zebra, it is able to eat grass that is too coarse and tough for most other grazers.

Lurking among savanna shrubs and grasses are a tremendous variety of insects, some of them as colorful as this gaudily painted grasshopper (above). While grasshoppers feed mainly on green, growing leaves, other animals such as the spring hare (right) depend more on foods such as roots and bulbs. Active mainly at night, kangaroolike spring hares spend most of the day unseen in their burrows.

HIDDEN HERBIVORES

No visitor to the savanna can fail to notice
the vast herds of wildebeests, gazelles, zebras,
and other large grazers. Yet these lush
pastures support multitudes of less conspicuous
creatures that also depend on plants for food.
Some of them, especially insects and rodents,
are so numerous that they may actually be
just as important as the larger animals in
converting growing plants into living animal
flesh.

*Several kinds of ground squirrels
thrive on the African plains. These
burrowers, especially fond of bulbs,
roots, and fallen fruit, sometimes
become pests where crops are
cultivated.*

*Termites have voracious appetites
for dead grass. Workers often travel
substantial distances from the
mounds as they forage for food for
the colony.*

Ruined pastures

If we were to drive further east outside the park boundary, we would come to places where Masai tribesmen build their homesteads, or *bomas*, near waterholes used by their herds of cattle. Here we would find a complete contrast to the healthy state of the plains within the park. In areas inhabited solely by wild animals, deep-rooted grasses usually grow to within a few yards of waterholes. But around waterholes used by domestic stock, there is invariably an expanse of bare ground up to half a mile wide, with eroded tracks radiating from it like the spokes of a wheel.

This is caused by the daily or nightly concentration of too many animals in one place. Wild animals are continually moving about and can graze at any time, day or night. Domestic cattle owned by people such as the Masai, in contrast, graze for only seven or eight hours a day and are returned to the same place each night for months on end. The Masai, understandably, do not want to go to the trouble of packing up and moving to another place before they must. They often continue to use a waterhole until it is dry, even though little grass is left around it. Thus they ruin the country in a way that wild animals never do.

Even the fertilizing manure of the wild animals is spread evenly over the country, while that of domestic stock is piled in vast heaps in the centers of the bomas. There it is left to rot, or it may eventually be burned or else sold to farmers by the truckload. In any case, the nutrients in the manure are never returned to the soil of the surrounding savanna.

Much of the manure of wild animals, however, besides being widely scattered over the plain, is actually buried underground. Throughout savannas, millions of burly, black, inch-long dung beetles perform an invaluable service by gathering fresh dung into balls and burying them. They lay their eggs in the dung, which serves as a food supply for their larvae when they hatch. Any manure that is not eaten by the larvae remains in the soil and becomes available as fertilizer for the grass.

A simple barbed-wire fence provides a study in contrasts. In the pasture to the right of the fence, a concentration of too many domestic animals has practically denuded the land of vegetation. On the other side of the fence, where fewer animals have been allowed to graze, the range is still in fairly good condition.

NGORONGORO CRATER CONSERVATION AREA

Only a few miles to the east of Serengeti National Park is another of Tanzania's great wildlife preserves, Ngorongoro Crater Conservation Area. The dominant feature of the 2500-square-mile conservation area is the huge crater of a collapsed volcano some nine miles in diameter and ringed by walls over two thousand feet high (*upper*). The floor of the crater, a mixture of grasslands, woodlands, marshes, and lakes, is populated by a wealth of wild animals such as the zebras and wildebeests in the lower picture. To the right, a flock of sacred ibises wing across a pond in the conservation area.

Because of its long slender neck, the gerenuk is sometimes called the giraffe-gazelle. A resident of arid brushlands, it browses on leaves and tender young twigs of trees and bushes. To reach higher branches, it easily rears up on its hind legs and braces itself against the tree.

To each his own food

The continuous movement of the wild herds and their migratory nature tell only part of the story, however. In addition, through years of patient study scientists have discovered that different species of wild grazers each prefer to feed on different types of grass or grasses at different heights or growth stages.

Observing the herds from our car, it is extremely difficult even at close range to tell exactly what a wild animal is eating. In the case of a browsing animal, which may nibble for minutes on end on one or two shrubs, it is easy to go over to the bush when the animal leaves and find out what it is. But when a zebra pushes its face into a patch of long mixed grasses, it could be eating anything—or everything!—in the patch.

To solve these riddles, scientists have developed a number of means for identifying the animals' food sources. When they first began studying the question, they sometimes shot

78

the animals and opened their stomachs to identify the plants found there. Fortunately this is no longer necessary. Although the grasses eaten by the animals are mostly digested, some recognizable parts pass through in their dung. Minute fragments of the epidermis, or skin, of grasses come through undamaged, and for each kind of grass the fragments look slightly different when examined under a microscope. Thus by merely following an animal around and collecting its droppings for later examination, we can get a very good idea of what it has been eating.

Of course if plenty of lush young grass is available, many animals may be found to eat much the same thing. But various studies have shown that in many areas each wild animal has its own food preferences, and these preferences are often nicely complementary to each other.

In one study it was found that wildebeests apparently prefer the green leaves and stalks of young red oat grass and a species of wire grass that is often ignored by cattle if anything else is available. In the same area Thomson's gazelles nibbled mainly on the fresh green leaves of star grass and

The giraffe, towering as high as eighteen feet, can nibble on leaves far beyond the reach of other browsers. But it does not disdain low-growing plants. Though awkward, it can stoop to munch on appetizing morsels growing right on the ground.

secondarily on guinea grass, but they ate very little red oat grass. Grant's gazelles, on the other hand, preferred shrubs and herbs. What little grass they ate was mainly of a species that is ignored by most other grazers. Most surprising of all, the topis ate the dried stems of star grass and annual needle grasses. Since they could just as well have eaten the fresh green star grass or red oat grass, which were plentiful, the scientists concluded that the topis ate the dried stuff because they preferred it. In this way they performed a very useful function, for they ate up the dry stalks and stems the other animals ignored.

Ever on the move, a line of wildebeests plods patiently across an African plain. In Serengeti, as the dry season approaches, these animals abandon the short-grass plains and trek westward to the park's long-grass woodlands, where they will find fresh grass and dependable water supplies.

Woodland pastures

Visiting the plains in January gives us only half of the picture of the life in Serengeti. To see the other half, we must return in July when the plains are dry and the animals have made their great trek westward to the long-grass woodlands of the park.

By now the short-grass plains are nearly deserted. When we were last here, we could see tens of thousands of animals in a day's drive over the plains, but now we see practically nothing except for some ostriches and a few herds of Grant's gazelles. These beautiful beasts, the largest and finest of all gazelles, range widely over the desert and semidesert areas of northern Kenya and southern Ethiopia. They can continue to live on the dry plains of Serengeti after almost everything has left since they need almost no water at all to survive. They subsist mainly by browsing twigs and leaves, but even eat the bitter yellow fruits of the Sodom apple.

The Thomson's gazelles, probably the most numerous animals on the plains in January, now are almost all gone. A few small herds may linger along watercourses where there is still a little green grass. But they are no longer dotted over the landscape as far as the eye can see. As we head north to the acacia woodlands around Seronera, they become more numerous. Here there are also fair numbers

of topis, which, as we have seen, can clean up dry grasses after other animals can no longer find anything to eat.

Going farther west or north, if we are lucky, we shall once again come upon the great herds of wildebeests and zebras, moving along steadily, never resting long in one place, until they finally concentrate in their dry-season grazing grounds, near rivers that provide a permanent source of water. These are the long-grass woodlands in the western part of the park, where tall red oat grass and hood grass make a carpet beneath scattered twenty-foot-tall acacias and combretums. As soon as we stop the car to look at the zebras and wildebeests, we realize that, while they are still the most numerous animals in the landscape, they now associate with many other resident species that never visit the open plains.

81

Plant-eaters everywhere

There are large herds of buffaloes, huge black animals that resemble cattle. Herds of several hundred feed together in areas of open grassland or, in the heat of midday, lie in tightly packed inky masses in the shade of big trees. Since they require good grazing, shade, and permanent water, they remain here where there are rivers throughout the year, never moving far out onto the plains. Although they have a reputation for savagery, they are actually very placid animals. They may come up to a car in a solid, black, menacing-looking mass—for they are very curious—but then they will suddenly turn and run off, flinging their legs and tails up behind like a troop of skittish calves.

Many herds of bush-loving impalas are also here, the males distinguished by long lyrate horns. These beautiful, bright reddish-brown antelopes are famous for their jumping power; they can easily leap as far as thirty feet in a single bound.

In more open patches of woodland we find many herds of hartebeests and topis, along with groups of elands. Here and there we may also spot small groups of the three hundred or so roan antelope that live in northern and western Serengeti. Horselike in shape, these handsome animals have

The impala's prodigious jumping ability is a useful talent in country inhabited by cheetahs, wild dogs, and other swift hunters. A resident of wooded savannas, it browses on the leaves of trees and shrubs, but sometimes eats grass as well.

black and white markings on their faces and sharp sickle-shaped horns that curve back over their necks.

Dark-brown long-haired waterbucks and pale-brown reedbucks frequent the long grass near the rivers. And in the rivers themselves, the massive head of a hippopotamus may from time to time emerge from the water and regard us curiously before submerging again.

In dense thickets there may be a few black rhinoceroses. Here too live bushbucks, beautiful red-brown creatures spotted with white, that tread about delicately, nibbling on leaves and buds. Many dik-diks, tiny gray-brown antelope that walk on pencil-thin legs, also inhabit the thickets, while on more open wooded grasslands there are bush duikers, so-called because of the diving motion with which they escape into thick cover. They are among the most widespread and adaptable of savanna animals, but like dik-diks and bush-bucks, they live singly or in small groups rather than in large herds.

Perhaps the most amusing sights of all are the parties of wart hogs that live near the rivers but are occasionally seen out on the open plains too. At the approach of our car, they run away with their tails held upright, the black tuft at the tips serving as flags that guide the young wart hogs when they follow their mothers through the long grass.

With tails held high like banners, a group of wart hogs flees in alarm. These wild pigs, widespread on African savannas, usually travel in family parties that include two parents and the young of one or even two successive litters.

THE AMPHIBIOUS HIPPO

Equally at home on land or in
water, hippopotamuses are
found near grass-bordered lakes
and rivers throughout much of
central Africa. By day they
sleep on shore or loll in the
water, where they rest with
their nostrils projecting just
above the surface (*left*). In the
evening they emerge from the
water to graze on the plains
(*right*), sometimes traveling
several miles along well-defined
paths to their favored feeding
haunts. Truly amphibious, they
can dive to the bottom of a
lake or river and remain
submerged for several minutes
at a time, resting on the bottom
or even walking around beneath
the water (*next two pages*).

The largest of all living birds, ostriches are seven to eight feet tall and weigh as much as 350 pounds. Despite their inability to fly—their wings are small and their flight muscles poorly developed—they can easily escape danger by running at speeds of over forty miles an hour. In this group sprinting at top speed across the dusty surface of a dry lake bed, the black birds are adult males and the lighter ones are females and immature birds.

Savanna monkeys

Hoofed grazers are not the only animals that eat the vegetation at Serengeti. As we travel through the woodlands we continually come upon troops of baboons. These large, long-tailed monkeys have forsaken the usual habits of their kind and come down from the trees to feed mainly on the ground. At night or in times of danger, however, they still take to the trees and rocks for safety.

The females and young are often scrawny, with rather patchy fur, but an old male with a well-groomed coat of long hair is definitely an impressive animal. Baboons travel about in mixed troops of up to one hundred animals, though groups of twenty to fifty are more usual. In the course of a day, the band may travel from five to fifteen miles, feeding in the morning, resting in the shade at midday, and eating again on their way back to their roosting place in the evening. They feed mainly on grass, but also eat other plant material, particularly figs. They eat many insects, and occasionally may even vary their diet with a young antelope.

In fact, because they are *omnivorous* (willing to eat anything, whether plant or animal) and because they have virtually no competition, they have managed to become one of the commonest and most obvious of all savanna animals. They are often disliked by human beings, especially since they help themselves to planted crops whenever they can. The fact that they survive in numbers even in densely populated areas is a tribute to their intelligence and adaptability.

Flightless wonders

Another characteristic animal of the savanna—and another varied feeder—is the ostrich. As we travel about, we see ostriches in pairs, small groups, or sometimes singly, out on the open plains, but seldom in denser woodlands. If we should decide to pursue an ostrich in a car, it trots off slowly at first, casting apprehensive glances over its shoulder. Its action, steady and even, indicates that it is not yet going at full speed. When we press it at thirty-five miles an hour, it accelerates briskly and moves ahead rapidly with a sprint that takes it well up to forty-five miles an hour. Outdistanc-

Startlingly similar to ostriches in general appearance are the large flightless rheas of South America (*upper*) and emus of Australia (*lower*). Like ostriches, both are powerful runners that have evolved similar adaptations for survival on open grasslands and deserts.

ing us, the ostrich slows to a trot again, and will continue like this for ten miles if we have the patience to follow.

From behind, the big bird looks irresistibly comical. But it is obvious that it is an efficient running machine. The ostrich is such a good runner, in fact, that it uses its plumed fanlike wings only for courtship and other displays and cannot fly at all.

The ostrich, standing eight feet tall, is the largest surviving flightless bird in the world. Others—rheas, emus, cassowaries, and kiwis—inhabit South America, Australia, New Guinea, and New Zealand. In the past there were also moas in New Zealand and elephant birds on the island of Madagascar, but these are now extinct. Most of the present-day flightless species inhabit savannas, where their long running legs are a useful adaptation, as they are for giraffes.

Giants of the plain

Anyone watching this pageant of wildlife in Serengeti's long-grass woodlands cannot help but marvel at the tremendous variety of animals all living together in harmony with their environment. Each one seems to play a separate yet indispensable role in the working of the savanna community. But when we examine their habits more carefully, we realize that two species—the giraffe and the elephant—are absolutely unique.

The elephants are likely to be seen almost anywhere—in thicket, forest patch, or open grassland—feeding roughly on trees or simply standing in the shade with their big ears swinging to and fro. They are so obviously versatile and intelligent that no one who studies them can ever be bored. As we watch from the car, they appear placid and imperturbable. But if we were on our feet, alone and unarmed, we would find that the elephant has a unique capacity: it can make a human being feel really small. Even at birth an elephant weighs about 240 pounds, while an adult bull, standing over eleven feet high at the shoulder, may reach a maximum weight of over 6 tons.

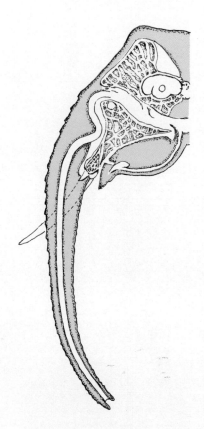

Though massive and consisting mostly of bone, the elephant's small-brained skull is not nearly as heavy as it appears. A network of open air-spaces in the bone greatly reduces the weight of the animal's huge skull.

A full-grown elephant feeds almost constantly, consuming 500 pounds or more of vegetation every day. Leaves, twigs, bark, grass, and even fruits all help to satisfy its voracious appetite.

When it is born, a baby elephant has no tusks, and its trunk at first is a useless appendage that has to be curled away over its head when it suckles for milk. The tusks begin to show when the elephant is about two years old, and continue to grow throughout most of its life. But it is its trunk that really serves the elephant well and makes it so versatile.

The elephant uses its trunk for feeding. It often wraps the trunk around a leafy branch and then strips off a bunch of leaves and twigs, just as we can use our hands to strip the leaflets from a fern frond. In much the same way it can grasp a clump of grass and rip it free. When drinking, it sucks water into its trunk and then squirts it down its throat. And it smells with the nostrils situated in the tip of the trunk.

But it also uses its trunk when playing with or greeting

other elephants, and even in making love. It is handy for steering a weak and wobbly baby about, but can also be used for chastising the young when the need arises. With the help of its trunk an elephant can shift large obstacles about, but using the two fingerlike processes at the tip, it can also grip items as small as a single acacia pod or a smooth round berry.

The trunk normally hangs down, slightly curled, in front of the animal, though a resting elephant often hangs it over one tusk where, in time, it wears a groove. In a normal adult the trunk is about seven feet long, but it can be extended like a concertina. By stretching it upward, the elephant can reach food as high as eighteen feet above the ground, about the same height reached by a bull giraffe. If necessary, the elephant sometimes gets at still higher vegetation by simply pushing the trees over.

Head to head, two playful young elephants engage in mock battle. As they grow up, young elephants never lack companionship, for the great beasts live in herds of as many as fifty individuals, although groups of ten or twenty are more usual.

Although all giraffes are identical in general appearance, five distinct races are found in various areas of Africa, each one distinguished by somewhat different colors and patterns. This one, the reticulated giraffe, lives in northern Kenya and Ethiopia. Its sharply defined chestnut patches are separated by narrow white lines. The Kenya, or Masai, giraffe, found in Kenya and Tanzania, in contrast, has irregularly shaped, tanner patches with the jagged outlines separated by buffy areas.

Long necks, long legs

Although there are relatively few elephants in Serengeti, there are plenty of giraffes. Among the acacias we regularly pass herds of them, reaching up to nibble leaves or sometimes bending down to feed on herbs among the grass. Long-necked, slightly bizarre, and yet supremely graceful, they are always fascinating to observe, especially since those in Serengeti are very tame.

In contrast to elephants, giraffes are delicate feeders. Ignoring grass and hard twigs, they nibble instead on green leaves, mainly of acacias, but also of other trees and shrubs. While elephants must eat huge quantities of food each day, giraffes can subsist on relatively little, since their diet is uniformly high in protein.

Despite their ability to feed anywhere from ground level to eighteen feet high, however, they have less effect on the vegetation than elephants do. Their constant browsing keeps acacias and other trees in check. But they simply prune the treetops; they do not push them over.

Giraffes seem especially fond of one species of acacia, the ant-gall acacia. At the bases of their thorns, these trees have hollow bulblike growths which are inhabited by ants. When the tree is touched, the ants swarm out and apparently deter many animals that would otherwise browse the leaves. Giraffes, however, take very little notice of the ants.

Although elephants are fond of other acacias, they do not seem to eat much of the ant-gall acacias. Perhaps they are discouraged by the ants crawling all over their sensitive trunks, as well as by the fearsome thorns. In any case, where this acacia is common, it is giraffes, and not elephants, that keep it in check. As a matter of fact, where giraffes have been exterminated or greatly reduced by ranchers, ant-gall acacias become dominant and soon greatly diminish the productivity of the grassland. Ranchers may not like giraffes because they kick down fences and drink scarce water; but without them, acacias are bound to become a problem.

Everything is eaten

As we observe the wildlife in Serengeti's long-grass woodlands and get to know a little more about their ways of life, we realize that each species has its own role to play in the

95

In the morning mist, a herd of giraffes thunders across the plain.

Cowlike, an African buffalo munches contentedly on a few coarse strands of grass. Buffaloes are never found far from water. Besides needing to drink every day, they enjoy wallowing in the mud.

functioning of the savanna community. We can also see that the way they work together to consume the vegetation is much more complicated here than it was on the short-grass plains. There vast herds of relatively few species—most of them grazers—consumed acres and acres of growing grass. But here there are about twenty different species of herbivorous animals, varying in size from six-ton bull elephants measuring over eleven feet high at the shoulder all the way down to tiny fifteen-inch-tall dik-diks weighing only eight pounds. And here there are many browsers as well as grazers.

It is doubtful if the relative amounts of usable fodder produced by bushes and grasses have ever been reliably measured at Serengeti, or anywhere else in Africa. But it seems obvious that, despite the cover of trees, grass is still the most important part of the vegetation here and provides most of the edible material. So it is not surprising that grazers, both migrant and resident, are still the most numerous animals and make up most of the biomass.

But the animals do not compete directly with each other for food. As on the short-grass plains, the habits of each species complement those of all the rest. Here, for example, the herds of migrant grazers that arrive in June benefit from the work already done by resident species in breaking down

the long grass. Buffaloes, more than any other savanna animal, can feed upon and trample down big areas of tall coarse grass. Near rivers, the hippos emerge at night and, with their hard, horny lips, graze the long grass down very closely in some places and leave other patches completely alone. As the smaller water supplies dry up, the buffaloes then concentrate near the rivers and eat and trample the patches of tall grass left by the hippos.

Even wart hogs have their own part to play. Unlike most pigs, they are grazers as well as rooters and like to feed on the short-growing grass in patches trampled by hippos. But they also use their leathery, typically piglike snouts to burst into thick tussocks of grass to reach the more succulent bases of the stems in the dry season.

Wherever savanna mammals have been studied in detail, it has been found that each one eats something different. In Queen Elizabeth Park in Uganda, for instance, biologists have tamed buffaloes, kobs, reedbucks, and wart hogs. By following the tame animals all day, they could observe from a few feet away and determine exactly what each one was eating. Although all of them preferred grass, each one fed on different species. The kobs, which grow to about twice the weight of reedbucks, liked to feed on short grass, especially

Like other pigs, the wart hog sometimes roots for bulbs and tubers, but it is primarily a grazer. It frequently drops to its knees to snip off short grasses with its sharp teeth.

buffel grass and creeping guinea grass. The smaller reedbucks preferred to stay inside stands of tall grass, nibbling individual leaves off the stems. Perhaps they felt safe from predators there, while the larger kobs felt more secure in the open where they could see around. In the same area hippos preferred star grass, while buffaloes preferred one species of *Sporobolus* and wart hogs liked a different species of *Sporobolus*. In contrast, a tame elephant, Samson, brought up in Tsavo National Park, Kenya, ate over a hundred different species of plants in one day, including grasses, herbs, and shrubs.

All in all, it is obvious that the twenty or more species of herbivores in northern Serengeti make the best possible use of the available food. Eleven of them, varying all the way from hippos to wart hogs and gazelles, are grazers. The grazers include all the most numerous large species such as buffaloes, zebras, and wildebeests. Five species, varying from rhinos and giraffes to tiny dik-diks, are browsers. Finally, four species, including elephants and impalas, eat grass as well as shrubs and herbs.

The result of all this is to ensure that no part of the

Plucking selectively with its pointed upper lip, a black rhinoceros has nipped off a coarse woody herb growing among the grass. Since black rhinos are primarily browsers, they normally are found in brushy areas rather than on open grasslands.

vegetation is left untouched. Everything is eaten, from the tops of the larger trees that are reached or, if necessary, felled by elephants, to tiny blades of grass only an inch tall. Fruits, leaves, flowers, and seeds are all consumed as they fall to the ground in shady places. Even the roots and underground bulbs of some plants are dug up by baboons and bush pigs.

As we look around, the vegetation may appear rather beaten up and knocked about. Actually it is fully utilized, but it is not killed.

Can cattle do the job?

The spectacle of the savanna means many things to many people. To the tourist, the sight of vast herds roaming free and wild through unspoiled countryside is reason enough for making the long, expensive journey to East Africa. But all too often when ranchers look at the scene, they see only wasted pastures. Why not get rid of the wild animals, they ask, and replace them with domestic stock? Besides being easier to manage, cattle and sheep would provide needed food for growing populations of human beings.

They go on to claim that domestic stock can use the varied feeding opportunities of the savanna just as efficiently as does this array of twenty or more species of wild browsers and grazers. Cattle, sheep, donkeys, and goats, they say, can do everything that buffaloes, gazelles, impalas and zebras do, and in arid lands camels can duplicate the work of giraffes.

The fact is that they cannot. The lesson to be learned from a place such as the northern Serengeti with its twenty or more species of wild herbivores, some migratory and some resident, is that each animal feeds on what it prefers. With such a variety of browsers and grazers, every sort of plant is eaten by some animal or another.

When only a few kinds of domestic animals are kept on the same kind of land, the situation is quite different. If there are not too many domestic animals, and if food is plentiful, a great deal of vegetation goes uneaten, simply because the cows or goats or sheep do not like it. When this happens, the undesirable species of grass in time become dominant and take over the area.

More often, however, the stock men try to keep more

Although black rhinos and white rhinos are similar in color and general appearance, it is easy to tell them apart. The white rhinoceros, primarily a grazer, has a broad, more or less square upper lip enabling it to crop off grass easily. The black rhino, a browser, has a mobile, prehensile more or less triangular upper lip with which it grasps leaves and twigs. In addition, the white rhino has a much longer head and a conspicuous hump on its neck.

BLACK RHINOCEROS

WHITE RHINOCEROS

cattle and sheep than the land can support, and the animals are forced to be less choosy. At first they eat what they like best until it is all but wiped out. And then they turn to the food they like less and eat that too, ending up finally with bare ground.

Nothing of the sort ever happens over large areas inhabited by heavy but varied populations of wild herbivores. Modern research has shown beyond any reasonable possibility of doubt that a given area of savanna can support a greater standing crop biomass of a wide variety of wild animals than of a smaller variety of domestic animals. And because of their varied feeding habits, the wild animals actually do less damage over all to the vegetation than do domestic animals.

Though surrounded by acres of grass, a browsing gerenuk chooses to nibble delicately at the few green leaves on a single woody shrub. It is only because each animal of the savanna feeds selectively in this way that the African plains are able to support such a varied assemblage of herbivores.

The Flesh
Eaters

Night has fallen two hours ago in our camp beneath tall acacias beside the Mwi River, a tributary of the Omo River in southern Ethiopia. Before dropping off to sleep, we lie contentedly in our cots, looking up at the stars and the flickering light of our campfire on the feathery leaves and branches overhead.

Somewhere in the trees a scops owl calls with a low, repeated trill. Frogs and toads chant from a pool nearby, their rhythmic chorus punctuated from time to time by heavy splashes as animals come to drink. Nearer at hand, a few crickets chirp brightly in the night. All seems peaceful, and drowsiness begins to close our eyes.

Then suddenly, without warning, a violent sound splits through the darkness, a series of deep, harsh, rasping grunts, each one preceded by an audible intake of breath. The call is so close, so loud and startling, that it makes our hair and skin prickle with fright. Even the oldtimers in our party sit up in bed, for they know the sound was made by a leopard. Will it remain around the camp, they wonder, or will it move off downstream?

We assure ourselves that leopards—the most beautiful, most elusive, for their weight the most powerful, and for their skins the most persecuted of all the great African cats —very seldom actually become man-eaters. All the same, the night is suddenly charged with danger.

Leopards are large and powerful *predators*, or animals that live by capturing other animals for food. For the baboons who went to bed in the tall acacias, gibbering contentedly among themselves, the menace of the unseen leopard is real: it can climb the trees to get at them if it wishes. So, with hoarse alarm barks, the old males of the troop begin warning other baboons in the area. The call is taken up by the deep crowing of colobus monkeys roosting on a tall fig tree downstream. All are anxious, for, apart from that one startling outburst, the leopard has been silent. No one knows exactly where it is.

At last the tension is broken by the loud doglike barking of a bushbuck two hundred yards upstream. It has seen the leopard and is fleeing, but at the same time is signaling the presence of danger to other dwellers in this part of the savanna. As if to acknowledge, the leopard calls again. But the series of deep grunts, even at this slight distance,

The solitary leopard hunts by stalking stealthily through the grass and then making a killing pounce when it is within close range of its prey. Although it prefers medium-sized antelope such as bushbucks and impalas, it willingly settles for game as varied as guineafowl, wart hogs, and domestic cattle.

seems less harsh and menacing. We turn over and go to sleep, secure in the knowledge that this leopard at least will not bother us any further.

Territorial signals

Since it advertised its presence so obviously, it is likely that the leopard was not even hungry. If we could see it in the dark, we would probably find that it is ambling slowly up the sandy and stony riverbed, with its tail carried high over its back in a graceful curve. From time to time it will stop, back into a bush, and leave a little squirt of scent at its own eye level. Occasionally it might defecate and, like a cat in a sandbox, scratch earth over its droppings with sharp strokes of its hind feet.

While these actions might seem strange to us, they are very meaningful to the leopard—and to others of its kind. By leaving scent signs along its route it is warning all other

The versatile leopard is as much at home in tall trees as it is on the ground. During the day, a favorite pastime is dozing on the stout branches of acacias, where its dappled coat blends well with the pattern of sunlight filtering through the leaves.

107

leopards that this is its *territory*; they should not intrude, for it will defend the area against all other leopards. The call, which so startled us and the baboons, probably was intended only to advertise its presence in its territory.

In just the same way, if we were to visit an Indian or Burmese savanna jungle, we would hear the voice of the tiger on its beat. As it walks through the jungle, the tiger periodically emits a deep, sonorous "Ah-aowm," sounding very much like a monstrous Siamese cat mewing in bass. Its passage is signaled by barking deer, whose alarm call sounds almost exactly like that of the bushbuck in Africa. If we were lucky enough to see the tiger walking along some cart track, we would see it back repeatedly into bushes, raise its tail, and leave a little scent squirt, just like the leopard along the bed of the Mwi River.

Odd as it may seem, the leopard and tiger are behaving just like a nightingale singing in a thicket, or a robin on a fencepost. Like the big cats' roars and scent marks, their songs warn other nightingales or robins to keep out of their home territories.

If we reflect, we will realize that almost all the sounds we heard before the leopard called were of a similar nature.

108

Apparently enjoying the sun, a group of lions surveys the landscape from a perch high on a rocky ledge. In contrast to leopards and tigers, which are solitary hunters, lions live in small communal groups, called prides, that may number thirty or more individuals.

The trill of the owl, the croaking of the frogs, and the shrilling of the crickets all have territorial overtones. They serve either to attract females to a male ready to mate, or warn other mature individuals of the same species to keep clear of a stretch of property that the caller claims as its own for breeding, feeding, or both. The effect of maintaining territories, as we shall see, is to keep individuals or family groups of any one species well spaced throughout their available habitat.

Whose land is this?

Tigers and leopards are solitary animals. They pair only to breed and otherwise live apart from one another. Lions, on the other hand, are social, living in groups, known as *prides*, of as many as thirty individuals.

The voice of the lion is the most magnificent of all, especially when uttered in a chorus. Even the roar of a single lion, on a still night, can be heard from four miles away. But at close quarters it is a shattering sound that makes the air vibrate. It begins with deep, reverberating, moaning calls—"mmmmmm-oh, mmmmmm-oh"—and ends with bass grunts that thud on the atmosphere.

To hear this magnificent sound, alone, unarmed, sleeping under the stars on the African savanna, is to obtain quite a new impression of the lion. You realize that it can be far more imposing than the rather indolent-looking creature, barely conscious of the ring of cars and clicking cameras of tourists, that we usually see in national parks. Lions roaring near camp make sleep quite impossible, and even after they move away, one sleeps lightly, starting apprehensively at even the rustle of a tiny animal in the grass.

The Swahili people interpret the lion's roar as *"Nchi ya nani? Yangu! Yangu! Yangu!"* And indeed you can make the phrase sound very much like a lion if you try. It means, "Whose land is this? Mine! Mine! Mine!" Thus, the Swahili people were wise, for this in effect is probably what the lions are saying to each other.

When they roar, they inform other lions of their presence in their territory, warning them to keep clear. In this way, frequent savage battles between the immensely powerful cats are avoided, and each pride can live more or less at peace with its neighbors. Although a territory is often defined as "any defended area," if powerful predators continually had to defend theirs against intrusion by actual fighting, they would too often be seriously injured. So they do it by sound, in just the same way as do inoffensive songbirds.

The mysterious leopard

Soon after dawn we set out to follow the leopard that called in the night and try to figure out where it came from and what it did after it disappeared into the darkness. This is far from easy, for the soft pads on the leopard's feet make such slight marks that they are difficult for even the most expert tracker to follow. However, a leopard likes to travel along well-worn trails. If we lose its tracks on stony ground or in long grass, we can often guess where it may have gone by looking around and picking the most obvious route.

If we are lucky, the tracks may finally lead us to the leopard, lazily sunning itself on a boulder at the edge of the

Although hard to find, leopard tracks occasionally are seen in soft mud. Like all cats except for the cheetah, the leopard leaves no claw marks, for it retracts its claws when walking. Its 3½-inch-long tracks, besides being smaller than a lion's 5-inch-long tracks, can be distinguished from the lion's by the two animals' manners of walking. The leopard's hind feet touch ground slightly behind the places where its front feet stepped, while the lion's hind feet land right on the marks left by its front feet.

FRONT FOOT

HIND FOOT

river or stretched out on a branch. More likely, however, this wariest of animals will have heard us coming and withdrawn to cover where it will watch our actions intently.

Leopards, in fact, are much more widespread and actually more numerous than lions in Africa. Although leopards are seldom seen, anyone who has walked twenty miles through savanna probably will have been closely watched by at least one leopard without having any idea it was there.

Today we are fortunate. Our tracker keeps with the trail and finally locates our quarry—a large male whose location is revealed by its long tail hanging down from the branch where it lies, twelve feet above the ground. The leopard is sound asleep with one paw dangling indolently from the branch. It is a glorious sight with the sun shining on its rich, yellowish coat, beautifully marked with clusters of black spots.

But as we crowd closer, eager for a better look, a stick cracks underfoot. The leopard awakens and turns to regard us with green eyes. To us they seem to have a hateful glare even if the cat's own emotions are only surprise and fear. Then in a single fluid movement it leaps from the branch into the undergrowth, where the silent mystery of its normal habits at once swallows it up.

With its kill, a forty-pound Thomson's gazelle, clenched in its teeth, a leopard eyes a sturdy tree trunk as if wondering what to do next. Stowed high in the treetop, its meal would be safe from marauding lions and jackals.

The leopard was not alone in the tree. Hidden in the high branches is the partially eaten body of a female bushbuck. When the leopard makes a kill, it usually places its prey in a favorite tree where it will be safe from lions, hyenas, and other marauders that might try to rob its meal. It climbs the trunk by gripping the bark with its claws, clenching the prey in its teeth, and stows the dead animal in a crotch among the branches.

Leopards feed on everything from francolins, partridgelike gamebirds that are common on African savannas, to animals as large as cow wildebeests. They hunt larger rodents,

The leopard solves the problem by making a giant leap. Clinging to the bark with its razor-sharp claws, it scrambles quickly up the tree trunk, and then . . .

. . still holding the gazelle by the neck, it continues to climb, bracing its feet against whatever support it can find.

Finally, the leopard reaches a secure perch where it can stow the gazelle snugly in a crotch. Only now will it begin to feed. What it does not consume at first sitting, it will return to eat on the next day or the day after.

baboons, monkeys, and nearly anything else they may encounter, but their preferred diet is medium-sized antelope such as bushbucks, reedbucks, and impalas.

Agile, powerful, and immensely adaptable, leopards are typically catlike in that they kill by stealth—a close silent stalk followed by a killing pounce. Once down, the victim is held by the throat until it dies of strangulation or dislocation of the neck. This may take a minute or two, depending on the relative size of the leopard and its prey. Our leopard, a big male in the prime of life, probably weighs about 150 pounds, almost twice as much as the bushbuck; in this case it probably killed its victim almost instantaneously.

Our tracker, a good climber, quickly scrambles up the tree to retrieve the remains of the bushbuck so that we can weigh it and estimate what the leopard has eaten. The bushbuck was probably killed two days before, and the leopard has fed on it twice, a large meal just after the kill and a lighter one last night. All that remains now are the head, forelegs, ribs, a bit of the back, and the bare bones of the hind legs. In all the leopard has eaten about half of the eighty-pound buck, forty pounds or so in two meals. But as long as we replace it, the leopard will probably return and consume another twenty pounds before the kill becomes too smelly in this hot climate and little is left but bones.

Then it will spend several days resting or wandering aimlessly with a full stomach. If suitable prey lets it come too close, the leopard may kill it, but it probably will not make a conscious effort to hunt for more food. Like other predators in their natural state, leopards are not wanton killers. Normally they kill only what they need in order to maintain themselves, which in the case of an adult leopard is an average of about six pounds of flesh per day.

A pride of lions

After breakfast we set out in the safari wagon to look for a pride of lions that lives not far away. The lions too have a territory, or home range, of as much as one hundred square miles, in which they always remain. But since they often travel several miles from one day to the next, they may be difficult to find.

After a big meal, lions frequently doze on their backs with their legs outstretched. Despite their sometimes playful appearance, however, lions can be dangerous and should be treated with respect.

We know that ours are probably nearby, for we glimpsed them three days ago as they fed on a freshly killed cow buffalo. Since they had not eaten for several days, they gorged themselves the first night and had consumed two-thirds of the buffalo by the time we found them in mid-morning. Each adult had eaten from fifty to sixty pounds of flesh, and all that remained were the larger bones and portions of the shoulders and neck.

After such a large meal, the lions were unwilling to move far. They had simply dragged the remains of the buffalo to the edge of an acacia thicket and had fallen asleep, scarcely visible in the shade. It was only when we drove past that one of them appeared, startled, and gave away their presence. But we did not get a good look at them.

Now, as we drive across the savanna, we keep looking for signs of the possible presence of lions. Vultures circling in the sky or gathering in a tree sometimes indicate a lion kill nearby; the birds are waiting for the lions to finish so that they can clean up the remains. And when grazers stare

A lioness is well camouflaged in the tall savanna grass, but when she raises her head, her telltale ears are warning enough to most prey species that danger is lurking nearby.

fixedly at something in the distance, the object of their attention sometimes proves to be a lion. If you look through binoculars where they are looking, a couple of small rounded lumps on top of a termite mound may prove to be the ears of an otherwise invisible lion surveying the landscape.

Today this approach works. About a mile from the buffalo kill we see antelope staring at some low acacias. As we look through the binoculars, a lion that has been resting in the sun gets up, stretches, and then moves into the shade and flops down. If we approach cautiously, we may be able to get a better look at the pride. As long as they do not feel threatened by us, they will probably stay where they are and allow us to watch.

Taking care not to disturb any of the grazers, which might bolt and thus warn the lions of approaching danger, we make our way slowly to a termite mound fifty yards from the acacias. And when we finally peer over the top of the termite hill, there they are, fifteen lions in all, and perhaps more beneath a small bushy acacia. One is an adult male, larger, darker, and heavier than the five brownish-yellow adult lionesses. The rest are cubs and year-old adolescents. The oldest of these are nearly as large as the adults and almost indistinguishable from them until they stand up and reveal the subdued spots on their undersides. By the time they are fully grown, the spots will have mostly disappeared.

A few of the smaller cubs are chasing each other about and stalking through the grass in comical games that simulate and train them for real hunting. The adults, satiated by their recent meal, are dozing quietly, lying flat on their sides and breathing regularly. For animals of such size—the lion sometimes weighs over 400 pounds and lionesses over 250 each—they are remarkably inconspicuous. From time to time one of the lionesses raises her head and stares into the distance. Lying on her belly, she can just barely see over the tops of the savanna grasses. It is easy to imagine how she could sneak up on unsuspecting prey. If an antelope or a zebra were to approach, she could flatten her conspicuous

As playful as kittens, lion cubs pass the hours in gentle play. The older cubs, on the ground, still have traces of leopardlike spots on their undersides. By the time they are full-grown, however, the spots will have disappeared entirely.

117

Learning by example, a group of nearly full-grown young lions watches intently—but from a safe distance—as a lioness goes about the serious business of hunting.

ears to her head and would then be scarcely visible from the front. If she wanted to stalk closer, she could move forward, like a snake, belly to the ground, hiding behind tufts of grass and in barely perceptible depressions in the ground. Whenever the grazing antelope raised its head, she would freeze to immobility and then move forward a few yards more each time the antelope lowered its head to graze.

Fleet as it is, an antelope has little chance once the lioness is within range for her final killing dash. Then she bounds forward in leaps of ten to twelve feet and reaches her prey in a second or two. If she misses with the first rush, however, the lioness gives up, panting, apparently aware that in a running race the antelope would easily outpace her. But if she reaches her quarry, she will pull it down and hold it with the fearsome inch-long claws on her front feet. Then she will quickly—though rarely instantaneously—kill it by strangulation or by breaking its neck.

King of beasts

Lions will prey on anything from guinea fowl to bull buffaloes weighing fifteen hundred pounds or more. Occasionally they even kill animals as large as a hippopotamus or a young elephant (more than likely, one that has become separated from its parents). Their favorite range of prey is large antelope and zebra of up to twice their own weight. From such a kill, a typical pride of one or more adult males, several females, and their young can take one large and one small meal, enough to satisfy them for several days. In all, an adult lion needs twelve to fifteen pounds of meat per day, more than twice the leopard's needs. But, then, a lion is more than twice as heavy as a leopard.

Having eaten a meal of fifty pounds each, followed by a snack of ten pounds or so, the lions do not need to kill again for several days. They usually lie around not far from their

In a desperate final lunge, the lioness pounces on a buffalo. She will kill the beast by breaking its neck or strangling it with her powerful jaws. The buffalo will provide a hearty meal for all members of the pride.

kill until they start to feel hungry and move on. As they digest their meals their bellies shrink until, when they are ready to hunt again, they appear almost as lean as greyhounds. Yet they are obviously solid masses of rippling muscle and bone, perfectly equipped for their task. If they fail to make a kill on the first day of the hunt, they can live quite well for several days more if they have to, just getting a little hungrier and perhaps ranging farther each day until the chance comes. Or, if they are lucky, they may be able to pirate a meal from a pack of hyenas or rob a burdened leopard before it can take its kill up a tree out of the lion's reach.

There are many tales about lions hunting as teams, with the males driving the prey toward a waiting ring of lionesses. It is more likely that they simply tend to be rather spread out while they hunt; when the prey flees, it is killed by whichever lion is in the best position to do so. Probably one

main advantage of living in a group is that, when a kill is made, it can be consumed quite quickly and guarded by a succession of lions while others go to water, instead of having to be left out in the open for vultures, hyenas, or other animals.

As we watch our lions from the termite mound, the adults dozing peacefully and the cubs playing, it seems difficult to believe that they might harm us. Yet lions undoubtedly do kill men, even in the best regulated of national parks. In contrast to tigers, which do not seem to become man-eaters unless very old or injured in some way that prevents them from killing their normal prey, man-eating lions are often healthy and in the prime of life. In certain regions, such as southern Tanzania, southern Ethiopia, and Mozambique, man-eaters are commoner than elsewhere. In such areas, you simply do not sleep out alone under the stars. If you hear their magnificent roaring chorus in the night, you climb into

While other members of the pride hover in the background, a lion gnaws the few remaining scraps of meat from the almost completely consumed carcass of a giraffe. Like most predators, lions are not wanton killers. They hunt only when they are hungry and consume their prey completely before setting out in search of another meal.

your car, wind up the windows, and lock the doors, or else you climb the tallest trees you can find and wait there until morning.

The lion lying under an acacia often looks mild and indolent. But he is not to be trifled with.

Normally, however, lions are afraid of even unarmed men; you can actually walk up to them and drive them off their kill. Lionesses with cubs will sometimes stage a fearsome demonstration, but they rarely charge home to kill. As a rule, humans have nothing to fear from lions. And the lion in turn fears and gives way only to human beings and elephants. Even so, it is with some relief that we back cautiously down the termite mound and go away quietly, leaving our lions undisturbed.

Coursing predators

Lions, leopards, serval cats, and caracals hunt by sight and stealth. Great speed is less important to them than the ability to move silently as a shadow to close range. Another cat, the cheetah, in contrast, is a courser; it runs down its prey in swift pursuit. The cheetah, in fact, is the fastest of all land predators. And in attaining this status it has lost some of the specialized equipment of other cats.

Although cheetahs are rare on the Illibai plains of Ethiopia, we might see one if we are lucky. If we could stay with one for several days, we would have a good chance of seeing it kill, for it normally hunts by day and is likely to attack its prey right out in the open.

One glance is enough to tell you that a cheetah is built for speed. It has a long rangy body and long thin legs. It is nearly as long as a leopard but much lighter and taller. Yet it can flatten into short grass that you would think could not hide a hare. Unlike other cats, its claws cannot be retracted and hidden in a sheath; only the dew claws on its front feet (the single large claws on the inside of the feet) are partially retractile, enabling it to hold prey when it catches it. Finally

A cheetah and her two cubs crouch behind a clump of vegetation and survey the landscape for potential prey. Easily tamed, these handsome cats used to be trained as hunters in Asian countries.

122

Although the cheetah depends on speed to run down its quarry, it first slinks up within easy range of its prey before bursting into the final killing rush. This one eyes a group of Thomson's gazelles, then . . .

its back feet are very large, unlike other cats, whose front feet are the larger. In this, cheetahs are somewhat similar to bounding kangaroos and hares.

The cheetah's body is dull pale yellow, like dried grass, adorned with round black spots. The ridge of the back is faintly maned, and from each eye a black streak runs down to the muzzle. These markings help break the cheetah's facial pattern when it hides behind low grasses.

Gazelles are the cheetah's favorite prey, although it can kill larger animals, and often preys on smaller creatures such as hares and dik-diks as well. An adult Thomson's gazelle can run for a mile or so at around forty-five miles an hour, and perhaps even faster over short distances. But the cheetah can attain bursts of speed of between sixty and sixty-five miles an hour. It can thus gain on a gazelle at a rate of about five yards per second, and, if necessary, will continue to pursue its quarry for half a mile or so.

124

By the time a cheetah launches into its electrifying rush, it will have stalked to within two hundred yards of a gazelle. If there is any cover at all, it can usually get even closer than this. When it finally leaps into full pursuit, it moves in great bounds, like a greyhound. Its body arches and the large hind feet strike the ground well in front of the head, while the heavy furred tail swings to balance changes in direction.

... with great bounding leaps rushes at its victim. Successful in her hunt, the cheetah then carries off the limp carcass of a female gazelle, probably to share the still-warm feast with her awaiting cubs.

Playing with a tame cheetah will tell us how it downs its prey: it clasps our ankles with its paws. If we were running, we would trip, and, once down, the cheetah would hold us there with its sharp dew claws. Like other cats, the cheetah kills by biting the neck and strangling its prey or breaking the spinal column. As far as we know, unlike lions and leopards, it never willingly eats what other animals have killed. But it may be driven off its own kill by a yapping pack of jackals.

Constantly on the prowl, wild dogs range over vast tracts of land and settle down briefly in one place only when their pups are born. Although they normally travel in packs of ten or twenty, groups of forty or more individuals are seen occasionally.

Nomads of the savanna

While the cheetah normally hunts alone, most other coursing predators hunt in packs. The coursers of the savanna include certain species of jackals and hyenas, and, most notorious of all, wild or Cape hunting dogs. These rangy, thin-looking animals, patterned with patches of black, brown, and white, are rather ungainly creatures. Their bodies are solid and cylindrical, however, and their legs are long and built for speed.

Although we saw hyenas out in the open on the Serengeti plains, we would be lucky to find wild dogs anywhere. They are such nomadic animals that you can never know where they may turn up unless you know the location of a den of cubs. The dogs sometimes return to the same dens year after year to rear their young, but otherwise do not maintain a permanent territory. Instead the hunting packs wander over great tracts of country. Their general ranges are much too large to be marked and defended from other hunting dogs, as a typical territory usually is.

Like cheetahs, they prey mainly on gazelles although, on the Serengeti plains, they also kill young wildebeests. Since their prey runs at about forty miles an hour, the dogs must be able to keep up this pace until the quarry tires. And they can. When running at full speed with their large ears laid back and their bellies almost to the ground, they no longer look awkward. Wild dogs travel at forty miles an hour without apparently being really stretched. The fastest human sprinter, in contrast, runs at about twenty miles an hour.

If we were able to follow a chase, we would find that the females are the dominant members of the pack and do most of the running and killing. The dogs often get quite close to the gazelles without unduly alarming them. Then they start to chase an individual that they think they can catch, perhaps because it looks a bit less fit than the rest, or is merely incautious, giving them a better chance than the others.

Once started, wild dogs do not often lose their prey. Contrary to common tales, however, they do not hunt in relays, with a fresh dog taking over as another one tires.

Wild dogs kill by pursuing their prey at top speed over long distances. Snapping at its flanks and belly, the dogs tear at the quarry's flesh until, exhausted, it finally falls. Although the dogs will settle for prey as small as rodents when game is scarce, even animals as large as this wildebeest are not match for a hungry pack.

What actually happens is that, as the prey runs in a curve, one dog will cut the corner with a burst of speed. Then, coming up from behind, it turns the quarry the other way so that another dog has a chance to do the same. When they finally get at close range, the dogs leap at the animal's flanks, tear open its belly, and bring it down.

They begin to eat their prey while it is still alive, and it dies only by being disemboweled. When the animal is a small gazelle, its agony, mercifully, is soon over. But with larger animals, the death throes may be more protracted. The victim is presumed to be in a state of shock and not fully aware of what is happening. Even so, a kill by a pack of wild dogs is never a pleasant sight to see.

The sentinels

Since they are faced with such an array of predators, all of them efficient killers, one wonders how any of the grass-

eaters manage to survive. For one thing, there is protection in mere numbers. Obviously there are more zebras, wildebeests, and so on than there are lions and leopards. And the predators are not indiscriminate killers; they kill only what they need in order to remain alive and healthy.

Mere numbers offer protection in another sense also. A great many of the grazers, as we have seen, live in herds. If we try to stalk a herd of hartebeests, for example, we will find that living in groups has definite advantages.

Approaching from the downwind side, and taking advantage of the cover provided by some small bushes, it is not too difficult to get within 150 yards of the animals. But to get within about twenty yards, as a lion must to make its kill, is not so easy.

For one thing, there is always a possibility that we may be spotted by a baboon. These monkeys can see as well as humans, with full color vision and sharp perception of movement and detail. An antelope may stare at a human being and then continue feeding. But not a baboon. An old

Towering above a herd of impalas, two giraffes stand as sentinels for the group. With their sharp vision and acute hearing, giraffes are quick to spot potential danger. If the giraffes trot off, the smaller impalas also flee without waiting to identify the source of alarm.

Thanks to its elongated face, the hartebeest can see signs of danger even as it nuzzles in the grass to feed. In addition, sentries usually stand nearby and keep watch while the rest of the herd grazes.

male will then climb to the top of a tree or perch on a rock, where he emits at intervals a deep, loud bark. Every animal of the savanna knows that this is the baboon's alarm call, and that it means a leopard, a lion, or some other source of danger is nearby. And they flee.

Ostriches also stand as sentinels for other animals. They regularly consort with antelope, and when the ostriches flee, so do the antelope. Their upstretched necks give the birds a view at eight feet, enabling them to detect danger over long grass or low bushes where some of the antelopes cannot see at all.

The warning systems are very effective. Antelopes take flight alike at the bark of a baboon, the sight of a running ostrich, or the sound of pounding hoofbeats of galloping giraffes or buffaloes. They know that these keen-sighted or tall creatures have spotted some danger, and they do not wait to find out what the cause of the alarm may be.

The many-eyed herd

Fortunately, however, there are no baboons or ostriches in sight today. Inching our way through the grass, we watch the feeding herd of about twenty hartebeests, including two sizable bulls. Omitting the calves, we have fifteen pairs of eyes to contend with—and there is almost always at least one animal with its head erect, looking around suspiciously while the others are grazing. One cow with a young calf seems especially alert and nervous. She is continually raising her head to look around.

As we watch the herd more closely, we realize that even the feeding animals seem to be looking at us. Hartebeests have curiously elongated heads, with the eyes situated rather far from the muzzle. This is a very useful arrangement for it enables them to see over the tops of the grass even while feeding on leaves halfway down the stems. If we pause to reflect, we will recall that several other savanna animals, wart hogs, for instance, have similarly elongated faces. In contrast, browsers such as the bushbuck and kudu, which do not put their heads down in the grass, all have short faces.

Attempting to get even closer, we try to slither, lionlike, through open grass. Wriggling forward, dragging with our

130

elbows and pushing with our feet, is not easy. By the time we have gone fifty yards, an old female hartebeest begins to stare fixedly in our direction, emits a sneezing snort, and stamps her foot. The rest of the herd immediately stops grazing and stares in our direction. We all lie still for ten minutes but the old cow is not satisfied. She turns and trots away. The whole herd then gathers and trots off for a hundred yards or so, where they turn and look back, several sneezing in alarm.

Clearly, living in herds is an advantage against close approach by predators.

But what about the large solitary bull wildebeests, hartebeests, and tiangs (also called topis) such as we often saw dotted about the Serengeti plains? Why do they stand there like sentinels, apart from the herds? And what are their chances against predators?

As we approach in the safari car, they seem to stand fast, unwilling to leave the place where they are. When we

With their horns locked in battle, two impala bucks fight to maintain possession of their harems of ewes. In many species of antelope, the combative males post themselves on small territories where they wait to mate with passing females, while rival males are driven away.

reach such a spot, we find a large trampled area covered with droppings, indicating that the bull has been there for some time. Then it dawns on us that this is his territory. Just as lions and leopards have territories that they defend against intruders, these bulls guard a small but nevertheless well-defined territory against other challenging males. That is why they are reluctant to move out of the way of approaching safari cars. The moving herds visit them in their territories, and there they mate with the cows.

As it happens, single territorial males of any species of antelope form only a small proportion of the total population —perhaps one in twenty or thirty or even less. However, predators kill a much greater proportion of males than this. In Tanzania's Ngorongoro Crater, for example, sixty percent of the Thomson's gazelles killed by wild dogs are males. It may be that even when approached by a deadly enemy, they try to hold on to their territories until it is too late to escape. In the same way, lions kill a greater proportion of the males of wildebeests, hartebeests, and topis than of the rest of the population of each species.

Obviously this territorial behavior is of no real disadvantage to the species. But it is also clear that, from the point of view of the individual animal, there is greater security in living in a many-eyed herd.

Safety stripes

To some extent many of the grazers are also protected from predators by their own colors and patterns. This may seem a little unlikely if we look at reddish-brown hartebeests grazing in fresh green grass. The tiangs, with their glossy dark-brown bodies and nearly yellow legs seem even more conspicuous. And in the strong morning sunlight, we wonder how anything could help but notice the vibrantly striped zebras, now washed clean of dust by the early rains.

Do zebras' stripes really act as camouflage as some claim? We can see how they might make the animals less conspicuous if they lived in groves of slender trees. But zebras do not live in groves; they live out on the open plains. How then can their stripes hide them from predators?

To find the answer we must return to the plain at night when the moon is high and full. The world now looks quite

The lesser kudu is a shy antelope that lives in thickets and rarely comes out into the open. It undoubtedly benefits from the light stripes on its coat, which resemble streaks of light filtering through the foliage and help break up the outline of its form.

different, for we cannot distinguish any colors at all. We cannot tell if a leaf is green or a flower red. Now we can look at the animals of the plain with something like the vision of a lion or of a dog or jackal, for these animals do not see color either. Even in daylight they view the landscape in shades of gray and black. Instead of looking for color, they are more attuned to movement. In fact, if you stand absolutely still, a lion will sometimes stare at you for moments and then look away, apparently satisfied that you are only a stump.

At night this places us at a severe disadvantage since we cannot see well in dim light. Lions and leopards, on the other hand, can see relatively well at night. Like house cats, they can greatly enlarge the pupils of their eyes to admit more light. Even so, a lion looking at a motionless zebra in moonlight probably finds, as we do, that it is much less conspicuous than the solid black bulk of a buffalo. The zebra's stripes, by breaking up the solid mass of its outline, probably make it less clearly visible to a predator. In the same way, the lateral stripes of gazelles and oryxes and the spots of giraffes help conceal them from predators lacking full color vision.

The zebra's bold stripes, by breaking up its outline, help make it less visible to lions and other predators. The spots and stripes of more colorful animals such as giraffes and gazelles also serve as useful camouflage, since their predators lack full color vision and see only in shades of gray.

133

The cattle egret regularly consorts with grazers, feeding upon insects that are stirred up as the animals move through the grass. Sometimes even hitching rides on their partners' backs, the egrets act as sentinels, flying up in alarm when danger threatens.

PEACEFUL COEXISTENCE

On the African plains, as in all habitats, many plants and animals rely on help from other creatures in order to survive. Such relationships, in general, are termed *symbiosis.* When both partners clearly benefit, the relationship is termed *mutualism;* when one partner is a sort of freeloader, neither helping nor hurting its counterpart, the relationship is called *commensalism.* Some symbiotic relationships are more essential than others to the survival of the partners. At one end of the scale of dependence are loose associations like that between ostriches and zebras or antelopes, in which the ostriches' keen eyesight protects the grazers from predators, while the greater number of watching eyes in the herd may be of some benefit to the ostriches. In this case, however, both animals can get along without each other. At the other end of the scale are partnerships in which neither member could survive without the other. Many termites, for example, could not live without the protozoans that inhabit their intestinal tracts and digest the cellulose in the plant food they eat. The protozoans in turn would starve if removed from their termite hosts.

Colonies of small ants make their home in galls on the thorns of trees known as ant-gall acacias. The ants help protect the trees by swarming over the muzzles of browsing animals.

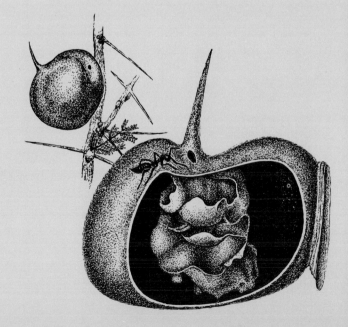

Like many termites, harvester termites cannot digest cellulose, one of the main components of the dead plant matter they eat, without the help of protozoans that live in their intestines. *Trichomonas macrostoma* is one of several kinds of protozoans found in the digestive tracts of harvester termites.

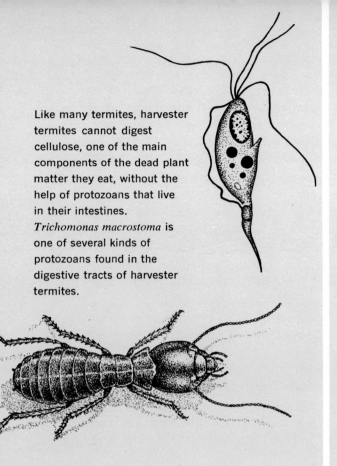

The seed pods of a common species of acacia, *Acacia tortilis*, are often eaten by impalas. The seeds themselves pass unharmed through the animals' digestive system, and in fact germinate better if they have been eaten and expelled by an impala.

During the dry season, the elephant benefits other animals by digging for water in the sandy beds of dry watercourses. When the elephant has finished drinking from the water-filled excavations, many other animals, from bees to rhinos, come to drink from the waterholes.

The oxpecker eats insects that it picks from the hides of large animals such as elands. Besides ridding the animals of parasites and warning them of danger, however, it sometimes pecks at open sores.

The undertakers

Not all the meat-eaters of the savanna are predators. Many are *scavengers,* animals that feed on the dead remains and wastes of plants and other animals. Insects and microorganisms play an important role in disposing of dead wastes, but some of the larger savanna animals also are scavengers.

Among the commonest are hyenas. We hear their loud howling roar frequently in the night. One evening their roars and high-pitched laughing cries from across the river are louder and more frequent than usual. In the morning we go out to investigate, and we find them—twenty or more—gathered around the carcass of an old buffalo that died of disease.

Hyenas are large animals; a big one is almost as heavy as a leopard. To most people they are far from attractive; their shoulders are much higher than their hindquarters, and their dull, yellowish fur, blotched indistinctly with black, has a dirty look. One or two of them are gorged and simply lie on the ground, their hair matted with blood. The rest are still tearing at the remains of the buffalo. Each time a hyena approaches the carcass, those that are already eating rush

An army of scavengers quickly clears the savanna of the fetid remains of lion and cheetah kills. Here, vultures patiently wait their turn as a hyena and two jackals tear scraps of flesh from a carcass. The ring around the dead animal's neck indicates that it probably had been marked for identification in a scientific study.

at it and utter high-pitched laughing calls as they try to repel the newcomer.

As the hyenas get down to the business for which they are specially equipped, we can hear the cracking of bones. Their jaws are so powerful that they can crush and break up all but the very largest bones. By the time they finish, practically nothing will be left of the buffalo except for the long leg bones, some of the backbones, the horns, and part of the skull.

Although this buffalo was dead when they found it, they would not have been deterred if the buffalo, though weak, were still alive. Once they found it, they would have begun eating it until it finally died. In fact, though it used to be thought that hyenas are strictly scavengers, recent research has shown that they are also active predators, able to kill animals as large as adult zebras. They can kill zebras only at night, when the wild horses cannot see well and cannot run at their usual pace. Other favorite prey are newborn

A seething mass of yapping hyenas practically covers a freshly killed carcass, possibly stolen from a lion or cheetah. The hyenas may even have killed the animal themselves, for scientists have recently discovered that hyenas are active predators as well as scavengers.

calves of wildebeests and hartebeests, as well as yearlings, which hyenas can easily run down. They sometimes hunt with wild dogs or, if they can, seize prey killed by the dogs before it is eaten. A large group may also drive one or a few lions off a kill, although the lions often turn the tables and take what hyenas have killed.

Hyenas live in large social dens, where the cubs are born and where they remain until they are large enough to join the pack and hunt. The dens, which may be occupied intermittently for many years, are the focal point of the territory held by a social group, or clan, of ten to one hundred individuals. Each night they patrol the boundaries of their territory to guard against intrusions by other clans. If

Like wild dogs, hyenas run down their prey in swift pursuit, with the pack snapping at the victim until they finally bring it to the ground. They can run at speeds up to forty miles an hour and are capable of overtaking zebras and wildebeests.

one clan has made a fresh kill that attracts rivals from another clan, the resulting battles can be ferocious. But the territorial principle is the same, whether applied by a solitary leopard, a pride of lions, or a large clan of hyenas: the defended area has to be large enough to support the animals that live in it, year in and year out.

Winged scavengers

As the morning warms up and the hyenas return to their dens, vultures often arrive to scavenge on their leftovers. Attracted by the trampled, bloody patch of ground, and the bones lying about, they settle first on trees nearby, waiting to make sure that no predators are lingering to pounce on them when they alight on the ground.

The commonest species in the Mwi Valley are white-backed vultures, which are widespread throughout African savannas, and Ruppell's griffons, the dominant griffon in tropical Africa. Both are specialists in consuming soft flesh and entrails. They get right inside a carcass, or push their long bare necks through narrow openings to feed.

While they eat often in throngs of a hundred or so, a few lappet-faced vultures and handsome white-headed vultures usually hover around the fringes, ready to snatch any pieces of meat they can. In time, two other species are also likely to appear, the small black and white Egyptian vulture and the dark-brown hooded vulture. Both of them are only half the size of the griffons, and they have thin, weak-

looking bills. However, they can make a meal of scraps dropped by the continually squabbling mass of larger birds, or by nibbling flesh off bones and hide and in narrower spaces where the heavier, clumsier beaks of the bigger birds cannot reach.

The Egyptian vulture, oddly enough, is the most versatile of all. It not only scavenges for scraps at carcasses, but also kills the young of colonial birds such as flamingos, and eats the eggs of flamingos and pelicans. Most remarkable, it is one of the few animals other than man that use tools: it smashes ostrich eggs by picking up stones in its beak and awkwardly throwing them at the egg.

Unlike the other animals we have been discussing, vultures do not maintain a territory other than a few square feet of space around their nests. They do not seem to really need any well-defined feeding territories. They are able to fly

Any carcass abandoned on the African plains soon attracts vultures from all directions. Soaring high in the air, they depend on keen eyesight to locate dead or dying animals. By the time they finish their meal, they sometimes are so gorged with flesh and entrails that they have difficulty getting airborne again.

so far in a day that they can usually find food when they need it, and, as long as they are not feeding young, can starve for several weeks at a time if necessary.

They have such acute vision that they are not likely to miss any potential meal as they soar at an altitude of one or two thousand feet. When they spot a large dead animal, or see hyenas moving toward a feast—or even another vulture planing downward to a perch—they gather from all directions for the feast. A feeding throng of a hundred vultures at a buffalo carcass, in fact, may well have collected from as much as five thousand square miles of country.

Walking oddities

Not all the meat-eating birds of the savanna are scavengers. A great many are active predators. Among the strangest-looking are ground hornbills, large black ground-dwelling birds with huge beaks and bright-red wattles. They move about in troops, uttering deep-toned calls as they make their daily rounds. Stalking sedately through the grass, they are constantly looking downward to see what they can find to eat. They live largely on insects, even digging up underground bee and wasp nests, but can also kill snakes and rats.

Another savanna predator that can fly but prefers not to is the secretary bird. Like ground hornbills, they are often seen walking around in short grasslands, although they generally avoid very long grass. The hornbills, on the other hand, are found in both short and long grass.

Secretary birds live in definite territories centered on their big stick nests which they build on the tops of giraffe-pruned trees. Here they roost at night, and in the morning they jump to the ground to start foraging. They walk through the grass at a regular two or three miles an hour, traveling many miles each day, even though they fly only to cross obstacles such as roads. As they forage through the grass, they occasionally run after some prey animal, or

The 3½-foot-tall secretary bird, so named for its crown of quill-like feathers, hunts by stalking through the grass in search of insects, mice, snakes, and other small prey.

143

HOLE-NESTING HORNBILLS

The turkey-sized ground hornbill, like the secretary bird, hunts on foot. Ground hornbills usually travel about the savanna in troops, scanning the ground for potential prey.

Hornbills, an unusual family of birds found in Asia and Africa, are readily distinguished by their enormous bills. (Since their beaks are composed of a bony network filled with air spaces, they are not as heavy as they look.) But hornbills are best known for their strange nesting habits. In all species except ground hornbills, the female walls herself inside a hollow cavity in a tree trunk at nesting time. Using material brought by her mate, she builds a wall of clay and dung over the entrance, leaving only a

small opening through which the male passes her food during the long incubation period. In many species, the female molts while incubating and is unable to fly if removed from the nest. In some species, when the eggs hatch, the female breaks out of the nest cavity and assists the male in feeding the nestlings. In other species, she remains imprisoned behind the wall and does not leave the nest until the young are ready to fly.

Clinging to a tree trunk, a red-billed hornbill passes a bit of food through a crevice to its mate sealed inside her mud-walled nest chamber.

Verreaux's eagle owl, standing about two feet tall, is the largest owl of the African plains. Although its favorite habitat is among the trees along water courses, it is commonly seen in less heavily wooded areas as well.

stamp rapidly to frighten out suspected quarry. They feed mainly on mice, but also eat grasshoppers and, from time to time, kill snakes, including the venomous puff adder.

Hunters by night

The most typical birds of prey of the savannas—or any place else for that matter—are owls and hawks. Although there are many species of each, they do not compete directly with each other, since the owls hunt mainly at night while the hawks hunt by day.

Sitting around our campfire beside the Mwi River, we hear the calls of many owls each night. If we were to go looking for the callers in the morning, we would find that the area supports quite an assortment of owls.

Downstream we find a pair of Verreaux's eagle owls, the largest of all owls in tropical Africa. Sitting side by side in the deep shade of a fig tree, they watch rather unconcernedly as we admire their soft gray and brown plumage. It is hardly surprising that they are here, since their favorite habitat is riverside groves of large acacias, with occasional fig trees where they can find deep shade. They nest in the abandoned nests of vultures and eagles, or sometimes take over the half-completed twig and stick nests of hammerkops, small frog-eating storks that are common all over Africa.

It is easy to tell what owls have been eating, since they swallow their prey whole or in large chunks and later regurgitate the indigestible parts in compact pellets. Beneath this pair's perch we find a casting of fur and bones that contains the incisor teeth of a mole rat, the skull of a fruit-eating bat, and the wing cases of beetles. Also lying nearby is the prickly skin of a hedgehog which the owls evidently peeled off and dropped before eating the animal. These big owls also prey on bush babies, large rats, smaller bats, frogs, snakes, and birds of various sorts, including other owls and large birds of prey that they presumably catch on the nest at night. Obviously they are not specialized feeders. They capture almost any small animal that is on the prowl at night. Yet, if they have to, they can get along on just beetles and small frogs.

Two other owls that we heard in the night, the scops owl and the pearl-spotted owlet, are both insectivorous. Both are

Skulls and teeth of African mole rats are sometimes found in the regurgitated pellets of Verreaux's eagle owls. Although the compact, short-legged mole rats are primarily burrowers, when they venture aboveground at night, they are easy prey for the watchful owls.

The magnificent martial eagle, the largest eagle in Africa, can kill prey as large as impala calves and young goats. This one is an immature bird about 2½ years old. In its full adult plumage its throat and upper breast will be as dark as its back.

hard to find, because they are so small. The scops owl, in addition, tends to perch near upright trunks where its markings and ear tufts blend so perfectly with the bark that it is scarcely visible.

Another large owl, with a sonorous hoot, is even more difficult to locate. But eventually we find a pair in the deep shade of a grove of big fig trees. Then we wonder how we could have missed them, for they are extraordinary creatures, with bright orange-brown plumage barred with black. We can search in vain for food remains beneath their perch, however. They are Pel's fishing owls, and they digest their prey completely—bones and all! Although no scientist has ever seen them actually fishing, we assume that they catch the abundant fish in pools of shallow water.

We are lucky to have seen them at all, since Pel's fishing owls are rare along most African rivers. Along the banks of this particular river, however, a pair nests every three or four miles. Their nightly calling, like that of all the other owls, warns others of the same species that they are present in their territories. However, a Pel's fishing owl will not be concerned if a pair of Verreaux's eagle owls, for example, shares the same grove of fig trees. They do not eat the same prey and therefore do not compete for living space.

Hunters by day

The trees along the river are the only really large ones for five or ten miles on either side, so it is natural that they should be used as nest sites by other large birds of prey as well. One nest that we find, situated on a branch of an acacia a little way back from the riverbank, belongs to one of the most striking of all birds of the African savanna—a bateleur eagle. These handsome birds, noted for their beautiful soaring flight, are specialized relatives of snake eagles, three species of which live along the Mwi. The snake eagles live almost entirely on snakes and lizards, as well as some frogs and occasional birds and mammals. Bateleur eagles, however, feed more on carrion and birds than on reptiles.

Another big nest, a great basin-shaped structure of large

The African fish eagle, never found far from water, lives primarily on fish, which it catches by swooping down to the surface of lakes and rivers. If fish are scarce, it will not disdain frogs, carrion, or the young of flamingos and other water birds.

With wings outspread, an African hawk eagle protects its young from the heat of the midday sun. The massive nest, built of sticks and twigs, is often used year after year by the same pair of eagles. Since the eagles add new material each season, the nest may eventually reach a diameter of six feet and be two feet or more deep.

sticks perched in an acacia on the edge of the open plain, belongs to an African hawk eagle. This black and white species is, for its size, probably the most powerful bird predator in Africa. Although its usual prey consists mainly of game birds, it is also quite capable of taking a young hare or a hyrax.

The next big nest we locate on our morning walk along the river, this one in a tree beside the pool where the Pel's owls hunt, belongs to a pair of fish eagles. These magnificent chestnut, black, and white birds live along all African lakes and rivers. They are common in forest and savanna country alike, as long as water, fish, and frogs are available.

The birds never go very far from their nests, roosting at night and resting at midday in the big trees along the river. If we were to travel a mile or so upstream, we would find another pair of eagles, and downstream we would find still more of them wherever there are water and fish. We even find nests along dry parts of the riverbed; apparently they are used in the rainy season when these parts of the river are full of water and fish. In fact, if we were to plot the nests accurately on a map, we would find that they are spaced along the available feeding territory with almost mathematical exactness. Where fish are really abundant, as in some of the larger African lakes, pairs of fish eagles nest only two hundred yards apart or even closer.

As we watch, we notice that the birds call whenever another pair of fish eagles passes overhead. The call, a loud ringing yelp that greets the earliest light of dawn and is uttered at intervals throughout the day, is one of the best loved of African sounds. But for the birds, it has special meaning. Their calling serves exactly the same purpose as the hooting of the owls along the river at night; it advertises their presence in their territory, warning off all other fish eagles and keeping the pairs well spaced through the available habitat.

A parade of predators

When we get back to camp we find that we have tallied between twenty and twenty-five species of vultures, hawks, and eagles, along with five different kinds of owls. Taken together, they feed on everything from large dead mammals

WAHLBERG'S EAGLE

MARTIAL EAGLE

The locations of the nests of Wahlberg's eagles and much larger martial eagles over 146 square miles of the Embu district in south central Kenya provide a clear example of territorial behavior. The nests of each species are distributed quite evenly over the available range since no Wahlberg's or martial eagle tolerates another pair of the same species near its own nest site. Because they do not compete directly with each other, however, birds of each species are willing to accept the presence of pairs of the other species nearby.

151

to guinea fowl, fish, and even small insects. Yet they account for only a few of the predators of the savanna. Besides the lions and other mammals we watched earlier, there are many small cats that are seldom seen, and a variety of carnivorous snakes, such as puff adders and mole snakes, which are probably important killers of young rodents in their burrows. In addition, fairly large animals such as aardvarks, which feed on ants and termites, and honey badgers, or ratels, roam the plains, though they are rarely seen and their habits are little known.

In all, thirty-nine different species of mammalian predators larger than a mongoose inhabit African savannas, or the rivers and marches of savanna lands. In addition, about sixty species of hawks, eagles, and vultures prey on live or dead animals by day, while at least twelve kinds of owls haunt the savannas by night. Besides many kinds of snakes, there are also more than two hundred species of birds that feed mainly on insects.

No other savanna area has anything comparable to the variety of carnivores found in Africa. India, for example, boasts both lions and tigers, but they do not occur in the same areas. There are leopards, too, and there were cheetahs,

The broad array of savanna predators includes several kinds of mongooses. Indiscriminate feeders, these weasellike animals dine on everything from eggs and young birds to insects, lizards, snakes, frogs, small rodents, and in some cases, even hard-shelled crabs.

though these probably are now extinct in India. But there is only one species of hyena, and the African wild dog is replaced by the red hunting dog, or dhole. Smaller cats, honey badgers, and mongooses are present, but there are fewer eagles and hawks than in Africa. Finally, some predators such as sloth bears occur in India but not in Africa.

In South America, the range of carnivores is even narrower. Leopards are replaced by the slightly larger jaguars and pumas, but the very biggest cats are absent. However, there are fewer species of large herbivores than in Africa. None are as big as a buffalo or zebra, and perhaps nothing larger than a jaguar is needed to prey on them. Although South American hawks, eagles, and vultures are even more varied than in Africa, many are forest species; the variety found in savannas probably is no greater than in Africa.

Do predators control their prey?

Faced with such an array of predators, we can see that there is hardly an animal, large or small, that is immune from possible attack, whether by day or by night. Just as the

The caracal, sometimes called the African lynx, is rarely seen since, like most cats, it hunts primarily at night. Easily recognized by its black ear tassels, this lithe predator is about eighteen inches high at the shoulder and weighs about thirty-five pounds.

savanna supports an astonishing variety of herbivores, each adapted to reach or digest different types of vegetation, there is also a unique variety of large and small predators adapted in various ways to cope with different habits on the part of their prey.

In all, as many as thirty different species of predators, large and small, may live in a few square miles without apparently competing with one another for food. However, the individuals of any one species are spread out evenly over a vast area and seldom meet each other at close range; as we have seen, each predator, whether bird or mammal, maintains and defends a home range, or territory, big enough for its own needs, or for its pride's or clan's needs.

Yet if we look at these home ranges more closely, we find that they often seem to be much larger than the predator really needs. Far more of its favorite prey species than it could possibly eat often lives within a predator's territory. Lions at Serengeti, for example, seem to have ranges of about one hundred square miles per pride, or ten square miles per lion. As we saw when discussing biomass, ten square miles may support half a million pounds of living animals—one hundred times as much as the lion's actual needs of five thousand pounds of flesh per year!

Of course, other predators kill some of these animals, and some of the grazers evade the lions by moving out on open plains for part of the year. But even if we considered only the lion's regularly favored prey, we would still find that there is far more than the lion could eat. The same is true of other predators. They all seem to maintain larger home ranges than they theoretically need in order to keep well

Alert but not unduly alarmed, a herd of wildebeests watches warily as a pride of lions ambles slowly past. Since lions kill only when hungry, most of the wildebeests and other grazers of the plains survive despite the toll exacted by predators.

fed. No matter how abundant the food supply may be, only a limited number of any one species of territorial predator can live in any area.

The answer to this seeming enigma probably lies in the fact that the prey in any such range fluctuates in abundance. Grass rats, for instance, multiply greatly in some years, reaching populations as high as two hundred per acre. And then they die out from natural causes and practically disappear from the area. Yet an eagle that feeds on the rats, such as the long-crested eagle, has to live even when the rats are scarce. If too many eagles lived in the area, they would not be able to survive when the rat population diminished.

In the same way, the lions in Serengeti remain in their woodland territories all year round. They do not follow the migrant grazers out on the open plains, for if they did, they would lose their territories to other lions. When the plains animals, their favorite prey, are gone, the lions have to subsist on the relatively few waterbucks, impalas, and buffaloes that remain, and sometimes go hungry until the migrants return and make their lives easy again.

Clearly then, the predators do not really control the numbers of their prey species. What they do, in effect, is to lick the cream off the top of the bottle. Despite all the predation, the vast majority of each prey species survives and reproduces. Their numbers are prevented from growing too rapidly not by predation, but by intermittent droughts or disease. Droughts strike the East African plains once every five years or so, and when they do, great numbers of wild and domestic animals die.

A hope for the future

All this has led many people to think that there is a large surplus here that could be managed and harvested for the good of protein-hungry human beings. *Game ranching* they call it. Why just let the animals die at intervals, they ask? Why not harvest them and sell the meat?

This is a rather new line of thought, and perhaps a good one. It is especially intriguing when we consider that, as we have seen, wild animals often utilize the savanna vegetation more efficiently than domestic stock and often do less damage to the habitat. As scientists try to understand how best to use land in a world where the human population continues to grow, they are looking more and more carefully at the possibilities of game ranching. The prospects are especially intriguing in areas where tsetse flies or lack of water make it difficult or even impossible to keep domestic animals economically.

Game ranching, in fact, may be one important way in which we can justify the existence of large numbers of wild animals outside national parks in the future. But the concept is still in its infancy. We still have a lot to learn about how to manage wild animals in their natural haunts before we can hope to harvest the surplus sensibly on African savannas.

The cheetah, a conscientious mother, keeps her cubs well supplied with fresh meat. As they grow older, the cubs will learn the art of hunting from her and in time will pass on the same skills to still other generations of cheetahs.

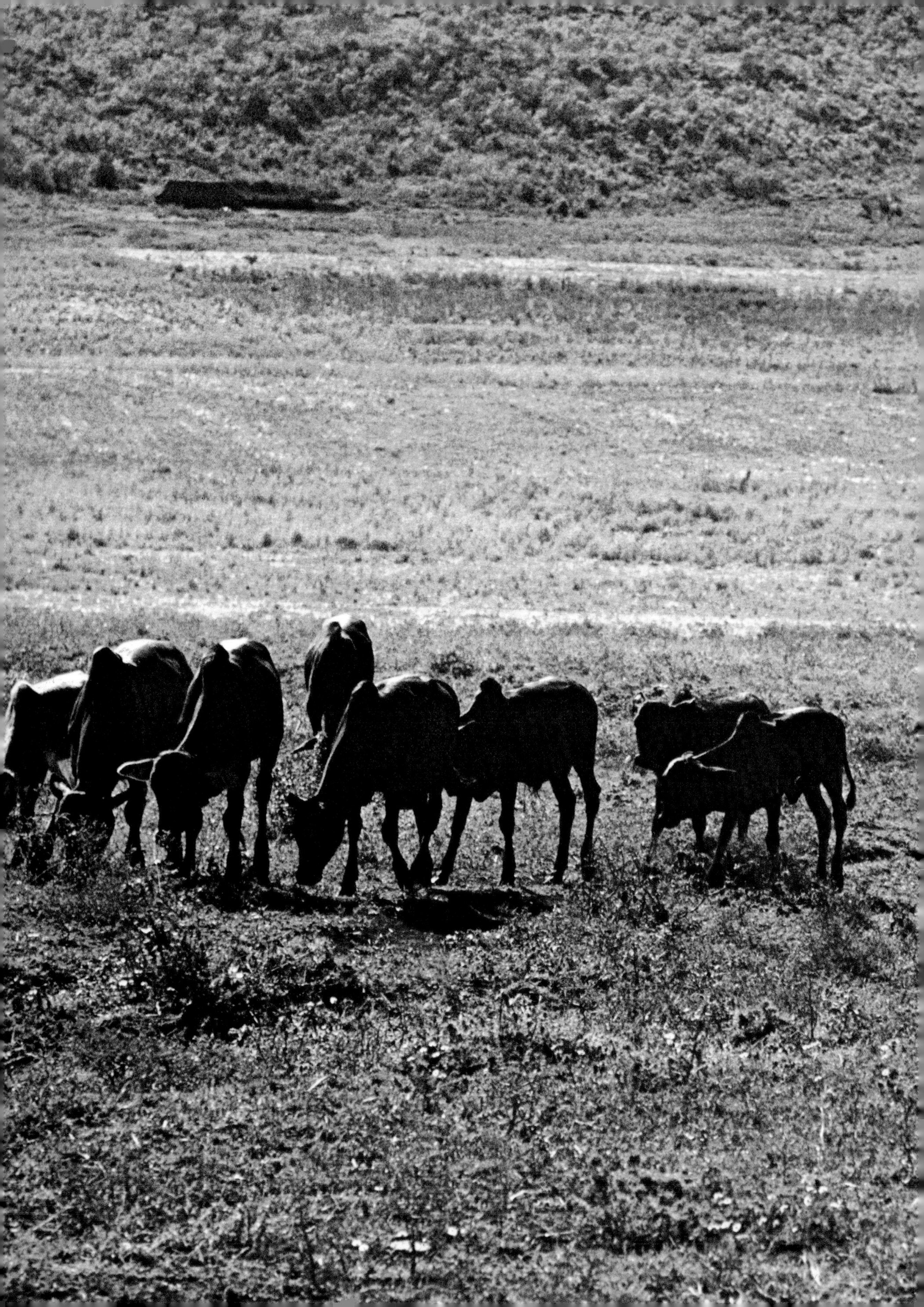

Men and Savannas

The evening before flying out of the Mwi Valley for Addis Ababa, the capital of Ethiopia, we take the safari car across the river and out on the Sai plains to the north. Then we climb to the summit of a mountain the game warden calls simply "Tooth," for want of any other name in this unmapped region. The immense empty landscape spreading south before us seems completely virgin and untouched, and as we look we sense the authentic breath of wild Africa.

It seems not only as if no men are here, but as if there never could have been any. We know this is not true because in 1939 a few Italian trucks trundled over this plain, and soon after, a column of British troops came through on its way to free Ethiopia. These events of the Second World War have been completely engulfed by time, however, and the landscape now seems totally empty of humans.

Nor do we see much wild life. Far out on the plain there are only a small herd of elands, some tiangs, and a herd of buffaloes emerging from thornbrush to graze. Then off in the distance we discern a few erect dark beings moving along in a line and we realize that they are men—naked black men,

Armed only with spears, a group of African tribesmen sets out on a hunting trip. Using their age-old methods of hunting, such men have little effect on wildlife numbers. But when they acquire powerful firearms, the result too often is wanton destruction.

each carrying a stick and several large gourds. They are Surma honey hunters making for their encampment in the dense bush along the river. Although we did not realize it, evidently they were here all through our safari.

Men in the bush

In the gigantic landscape they look as minute as ants. But they seem to belong here. They take us back ten thousand years in time to the days when the people who walked the earth were primitive hunters and food gatherers living on what they could find or kill.

When we look through a telescope, however, our first illusion of completely primitive people is dispelled, for one of the men carries a rifle and their gourds are too big to be of wild varieties. Yet for the moment, we can forget about these signs of modern civilization, since the lives of these people really are not so far removed from those of the

hunters and food gatherers of old. They are naked except for a string or two made of natural fibers and perhaps hide sandals to protect their feet from thorns. They camp wherever they want to in the bush and are self-sufficient as they move from one temporary dwelling to another.

If it were not for the man with the rifle, we could accept their presence without anxiety. Without the gun they can do little real harm to the area's wildlife. But with it they can kill the leopard that we heard in the night for the sake of its skin, or they can slaughter a buffalo for meat. Unfortunately, they usually select young females because they are more tender and easier to kill than old bulls. When many hunters kill selectively in this way, slaughtering an undue proportion of the calf-bearing young cows, they ultimately reduce the species as a whole by diminishing its reproductive potential. Equipped with firearms that they can obtain from technological men who live far away, these people can disrupt the balance between men and animals that existed all over Africa until the beginning of this century.

THE POACHING PROBLEM

Poaching, the illegal hunting of protected wildlife, is a serious problem in many African national parks. Seeing great herds of grazers apparently going to waste, protein-hungry Africans are often tempted to kill the animals for meat. Now modern commerce has further compounded the problem. Because high prices are paid for fur coats and other luxuries, Africans sometimes try to supplement their meager incomes by killing leopards, crocodiles, and other animals for their skins and hides, and by shooting elephants for the sake of their ivory tusks. Since the areas to be patrolled are so vast, it is often difficult to catch poachers in the act, yet African governments are working hard to enforce the laws. In the long run, however, the best course is to educate the people to the value of preserving their wildlife. People in other countries also can help by refusing to buy products made from the skins and tusks of endangered animals.

Wire snares like this one being inspected by a game warden are a sure sign that poachers are in the vicinity. Snares are a particularly cruel method of trapping, since an animal caught in one often struggles for hours or even days before it finally dies of exhaustion or loss of blood.

After a patient search, game wardens have found the camp from which a group of poachers have been conducting their illegal operations. Below, on the opposite page, one of the game wardens has placed the culprits in handcuffs, before taking them off to jail (right). Below, on this page, one of the poachers sits before the hideout surrounded by the group's illegal cache of meat and skins.

The bird and the badger

Sitting on our rock we have not until now noticed a small bird chattering in an agitated way in the trees just below us. Brownish above, yellowish below, and with a black throat, it makes a noise like someone rapidly rattling matches in a match box. At first we think we might be near its nest, but when we move off, it follows, chattering even more urgently. It is a black-throated honey guide, and if we follow it, it will undoubtedly lead us to bees and honeycomb.

They will probably be wild bees nesting in a cleft among rocks or in a hollow tree. If we attempt to rob the hive we will certainly be badly stung. But the men we have seen on the plain would welcome the arrival of the bird. In fact, if it did not appear, they would spread out over the ridges and whistle, grunt, or strike the trees with sticks to attract the bird. Then they would follow and, locating the nest, would smoke out the angry insects. Apparently scarcely bothered by the stings, they would remove the honeycomb and pack it in a large gourd for transport. They would leave a little comb for the bird that guided them and the bird would eat first the grubs in the cells and then the wax itself.

Although there are eleven species of honey guides in all, the black-throated honey guide is the only one that regularly leads men to honey. It is so widespread and characteristic

The immature black-throated honey guide lacks the dark throat which characterizes the adult male. Fond of bee grubs and the wax of honeycombs, these birds can easily be attracted to homes by hanging a section of honeycomb on a branch.

of most African savannas that many wild animals take its honey call as infallible warning of man's presence. A bull buffalo resting in a small patch of brush, for example, immediately rises and leaves when the honey guide calls. The men we saw on the plain would welcome the bird if they were seeking honey; but if they were stalking a herd of buffaloes, they would curse it and try to drive it away, though usually to no avail. The honey guide does not know when it is wanted and when it is not. It simply regards all men as a potential source of food if only it can induce them to follow.

This unusual association between men and honey guides probably derives from a still earlier association between the bird and the honey badger, or ratel. This dog-sized, low-slung gray and black animal is a member of the weasel family although it resembles the northern wolverine rather than the lighter European badger. For its size it is probably the most powerful animal in Africa, if not in the world, and is said to be able to kill animals as large as wildebeests. While it eats almost anything, it prefers honey and bee larvae and pupae. Secure in very thick loose skin that protects it from bee stings, it fearlessly climbs trees and uses its powerful tearing claws to break open hollows in trees to get at the hives.

Very few people have ever actually seen a ratel following a honey guide to a bees' nest. But African honey hunters

The honey badger, or ratel, is the honey guide's partner in getting at beehives in the wild. By chattering and fluttering about, the bird attracts the badger's—or a man's—attention and leads it to the hive. The badger then rips open the hive and both animals have a feast.

who claim to have regularly seen this sometimes grunt like a ratel to attract the bird. And it works. So we can assume that the bird does indeed guide the badger to bees' nests. Man apparently picked up this useful bit of knowledge either from the badger or perhaps from baboons which also occasionally follow honey guides. When we see this strange association between men and honey guides, we have an authentic glimpse of how, long ago, our forebears lived and found food in the African savannas.

Human scavengers

Indeed, if we could go back in time and perch ourselves on the top of Tooth in the year 8000 BC, we would look out over a vast lake instead of the sea of grass we see today. With a water level probably at least two hundred feet above the present level of Lake Rudolf, into which the Omo River now flows, the shoreline came right up to the lower spurs of our mountain.

Around the shores there were certainly men. They lived in encampments beside the lake, perhaps in caves or grass huts. Since traces of such camps have not been found elsewhere, we assume that these people lived mostly near water. Besides fish and fresh-water clams, they ate tortoises, croco-

Two million years ago the African savannas were home to many strange animals that have since become extinct. *Chalicotheres*, a member of a family of grazing animals about the size of large horses, had claws that it may have used to rip up grass. The antlered *Sivatherium*, about as tall as a modern giraffe, was a relative of the giraffe, though not one of its direct ancestors. . . .

Sivatherium

Chalicothere

diles, and many species of antelope and other grazers from the surrounding country. Although rains were more plentiful then than they are now in this rather dry savanna, most of the animals whose bones we find around the encampments were the same ten thousand years ago as they are today.

If we went still further back in time, to about two million years ago, we would find a much more varied array of wild animals. The elephantlike *Dinotherium* lived here then, along with several kinds of great pigs much larger than those we know today. Several kinds of hippos, some much larger than present-day hippos, shared the area with a number of species of giraffes, as well as camels, more than one species of wild horse, and many antelope. The predators, besides animals like present-day lions and leopards, included spectacular saber-toothed tigers. Although the primitive men who lived then had little defense against these great beasts, they apparently hunted them successfully. Or perhaps they lived more by scavenging—collecting and eating parts of animals killed by lions or saber-toothed tigers.

At that time, two million years ago, two species of men or near-men lived in the area. One was *Australopithecus boisei*, or Nutcracker Man. A skull of this creature was first discovered in 1959 at Olduvai Gorge in the eastern Serengeti, while others, or portions of others, have been found in the Omo Valley and along Lake Rudolf. Nutcracker Man, only

. . . *Notochoerus* was a giant pig, nearly as large as a hippo. *Dinotherium*, distantly related to the slightly larger elephant, had odd down-curved tusks. Their function has been a puzzle to scientists—one theory is that the animal used them to pull down tree branches when browsing. The huge baboon *Simopithecus*, as big as a male gorilla, was the largest known primate. Lack of enough food may have caused such giants to die out.

Dinotherium

Notochoerus

Simopithecus

THE SEARCH FOR MAN'S ANCESTORS

Near the western edge of Ngorongoro Crater Conservation Area in Tanzania, the plains are bisected by a barren, steep-walled valley called Olduvai Gorge. Although not very inviting in appearance, the area is world famous, for it is here that Dr. Louis Leakey and his wife, Mary, have made several discoveries of the fossil remains of some of man's oldest ancestors. One of their greatest finds occurred in July 1959 when Mary Leakey uncovered a fragment of a jaw that contained huge molar teeth but was unmistakably human in appearance. With painstaking care, the team of scientists excavated the jaw and other bone fragments. The result of their efforts was a nearly complete skull of *Australopithecus*, or Nutcracker Man, one of the earliest links in the chain of human evolution. Careful tests have established the age of the fossil skull at about 1,750,000 years.

Oblivious of heat that sometimes reaches 110 degrees, Dr. Louis Leakey and his chief African assistant work with infinite patience to remove debris, bit by bit, from fragments of fossil bone that later proved to be parts of the skull of Australopithecus or Nutcracker Man.

Working with a soft brush, Mary
Leakey dusts debris from fragments
of the Australopithecus skull
(right). Below, Dr. Leakey picks
away at the dirt to uncover the two
halves of the creature's palate. It
was the extremely large molars in
the upper jaws that first attracted
Mary Leakey's attention.

Back at camp, Dr. and Mrs. Leakey
sort the skull fragments they have
uncovered and then attempt to fit
them together like the pieces of a
puzzle. At the left, they have just
joined the two halves of the palate.
Eventually they uncovered enough
fragments to reconstruct much of
the skull of Australopithecus
(below). Although Nutcracker
Man became extinct about one
million years ago, elsewhere—
possibly on the African plains—
other humanlike creatures
continued to evolve into forms
more like modern man.

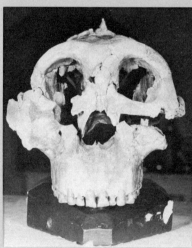

about, five feet tall, was probably not a carnivore, but a specialized vegetarian with very powerful jaws and teeth.

The other species, a more slender, more advanced, man-like creature is called *Homo habilis*, or Handy Man. He was so called because he made tools of stone or other suitable materials. With these he managed to cut up the carcasses of animals he found or killed.

Nutcracker Man died out about a million years ago. Perhaps like the giant pigs, giant hippos, and other monstrous animals that lived alongside him, he just could not find enough suitable vegetation to survive. Handy Man, with a more varied diet, did survive, however, and eventually evolved into the men living on the shores of the lake ten thousand years ago. It is not likely that these men were direct ancestors of the Surma honey hunters we watched. But it is certain that in their way of life as hunters, fishermen, scavengers, and food gatherers, they were not very different from some of the people living around Lake Rudolf today.

Pastoral man

Not very far away we can witness the next stage up the ladder of human development. Across the Omo River in the Gemu-Gofa province of Ethiopia and farther to the east, in Borena, the savannas are populated by *pastoralists*, herdsmen who keep domestic stock. Instead of using bread, sugar, or tea, they live on the meat, milk, and blood of their herds of animals.

Oddly enough, although the African savannas and sub-deserts are nowadays the home of the more famous pastoral tribes such as the Masai, Somali, Boran, Fulani, or Tuareg, the domestication of animals did not originate in Africa. The ancient Egyptians tried to domesticate both gazelles and desert scimitar-horned oryxes. But from their time to this, no really successful efforts have been made to domesticate any wild African species. Probably it was possible for early men in Africa to go on living as hunters and food gatherers without any need for domestic animals.

Farther to the north in Europe and Asia, however, things were different. With harsh winters and fewer wild animals,

Tending cattle, goats, sheep, and other domestic livestock provides a more dependable livelihood than hunting and gathering wild foods, and this is the way of life that has been adopted by a great many Africans living on savannas. These cattle are being herded across the Serengeti plains in Tanzania.

African pastoralists typically live in villages called manyattas, or kraals, with their mud-plastered houses connected by fences of upright branches to form an enclosure similar to a corral. During the day the cattle are driven out on the plains to graze, but at night they are kept within the manyatta where they are safe from predators.

it was none too easy to find enough to eat while simply wandering. So men there tamed and used camels, oxen, sheep, goats, and dogs. Eventually—but only within the past few thousand years—these domesticated animals were brought into Africa with successive human migrations.

This has meant that since the domestic animals are not native to Africa, they are not immune or resistant to diseases prevalent in Africa, though the wild animals are. By the same token, the wild animals are not resistant to certain cattle diseases introduced from Asia. Rinderpest, or cattle plague, for instance, virtually wiped out many species of wild animals at the end of the nineteenth century. Eventually both wild and domestic animals may adjust to each other's diseases. But in the meantime domestic stock is excluded from areas such as the Omo Valley where tsetse flies carry the deadly trypanosomiasis, while hordes of wild animals die whenever rinderpest breaks out among herds of domestic animals.

Even so, the pastoralists continue to make a living. The Boran, Hamarkokke, and Gelubba tribesmen who live in this area keep herds of camels, goats, sheep, and cattle, as well as asses to carry their goods when they move from place to place and dogs to help guard the cattle kraals, or bomas, at

night. So far these people have hardly been touched by twentieth-century progress, so it is an ideal area to see how they live and survive.

The milk drinkers

The lives of pastoralists center on their cattle. The cows are milked morning and evening, and graze only from about nine or ten in the morning until about six at night. During the day, the young men of the family tend the cattle on the pasture, while smaller boys and girls may guard the flocks of sheep and goats.

When the cows come home at night, the scene is one of bustle and excitement. Cows that have been away all day look anxiously for their calves, and the calves run about bleating as they search for their mothers. But they are not allowed to suckle at once, for the human owners must have first chance, collecting the milk in gourds. By the time the calves are allowed to feed, they are almost frantic with hunger. All too often not enough milk has been left for them, so that they are starved and stunted from birth and never grow into good quality cattle.

175

Milk is the staple of the pastoralist's diet. Sometimes, however, he supplements this basic food by drawing blood from the neck of a cow . . .

If a calf dies from disease, as often happens, the people are not much concerned if it was a bull calf. If they are very hungry, they may eat the meat, or they may simply leave it for hyenas and vultures. But if a female dies, the loss is more serious, for a female would have grown into a milk-producing cow. In fact, if we look at any herd, we will see that at least half or more of the animals are adult females, which these people consider their real wealth. Males are sometimes killed for occasional feasts, but females are seldom or never killed or even sold.

This is only sensible since the pastoralists, like other human beings, must eat every day. Unlike lions or leopards, they cannot gorge on meat one day and then starve for a week. Since milk is the only product of their animals that is available every day, it provides their main source of food. Each adult in the boma, in fact, drinks five or six pints of milk a day.

In addition, they occasionally drink blood, usually mixed with milk. The Boran of southern Ethiopia do not normally do this, for many of them are Moslems and their religion

... mixing it with milk (*left*), and then drinking the nutritious blend (*below*). In the dry season, when milk is scarce, the pastoralist fulfills his need for protein by increasing his intake of meat.

prohibits such fare. But farther to the south, along the Uganda border, the Turkana and the Karamojong regularly depend on blood for subsistence. Although the Masai of Kenya and Tanzania are more famous for blood drinking, they actually do not drink as much blood as the Turkana and Karamojong.

To obtain blood, an ox or cow in good condition is tethered and a cord is tightened around its neck so that the large veins stand out. An arrow with a tubular head is then fired into the distended vein, and blood flows through the tube into a gourd. When enough blood has been collected, the arrow is removed, and the cord is loosened. The muscular walls of the vein then close and the bleeding stops. Just as it does not greatly harm a human blood donor to give up a pint of blood, an ox can easily yield several pints at a time. Exactly how often this can be done safely, we do not know, but many of the pastoralists' cattle have scars on their necks, indicating that they have been bled repeatedly.

During the rainy season, when the pastures are lush and

Too many cows and donkeys lead to overtaxed water supplies as well as overgrazed land.

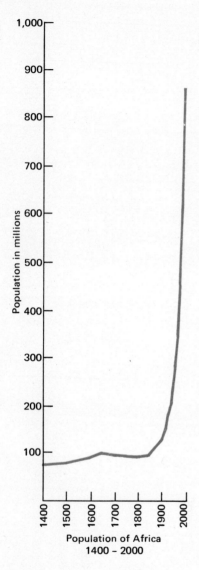

Population in millions

1,000 —
900 —
800 —
700 —
600 —
500 —
400 —
300 —
200 —
100 —

1400 1500 1600 1700 1800 1900 2000

**Population of Africa
1400 – 2000**

For many centuries the population of Africa, like that of the world as a whole, increased only slowly, but now it has begun to grow at a rate that threatens the future of the continent's natural resources. Based on current growth rates, it is estimated that the population of Africa will reach 860 million by the year 2000.

the cows are giving milk freely, no one drinks anything else. But during the long dry season, the milk flow dries up and the people are forced to eat more meat. This is the time when surplus male cattle are slaughtered for food. When a bull is killed, the owner usually invites other families to share the feast before the animal can putrefy in the heat. For single family meals, goats or sheep are killed and consumed in a couple of days.

Territorial men

In order to meet their year-round needs for milk and meat, a family of pastoral herdsmen—usually about eight people—obviously has to keep quite a few animals. On the average they actually need from twelve to sixteen milking cows, plus young females to replace old cows that die. In addition, they need a couple of bulls, several young males, and a number of sheep and goats for occasional meals of meat.

In all, such a family of eight must have about forty cattle of all ages, plus twenty or thirty goats and sheep to keep themselves alive all year round. If they have less than this they starve. And in any really dry year, which may mean every five years or so, they do starve, because the milk dries up and many animals die. As a result, every pastoral family tries to keep more than the bare minimum necessary for survival.

To protect itself from shortages, then, our family might have forty-five cattle and fifty goats and sheep. But to keep so many animals requires a lot of land. Although the carrying capacity varies in different areas, in southern Ethiopia a herd of this size would need about 250 acres. This means that only two and a half families can live on a square mile here. And if they are to survive, these people must protect their land from acquisitive neighbors.

Actually, among pastoral people, individual families do not normally try to defend their land. Families are usually grouped into clans, or sections of a tribe, which have rights over traditional grazing areas. As recently as fifty years ago, the young men of such a clan would, if necessary, battle with neighboring clans to defend their tribal grazing rights. Although such fighting has now been stopped in most of Africa, it still continues sporadically in southern Ethiopia.

180

In this the tribesmen are clearly similar to wild predators of the savanna. Like lions and leopards, they must maintain and defend a territory large enough to support all members of the clan from year to year. Nowadays they are faced with new problems. Just like agricultural people, the pastoral tribes are growing in number. As human populations increase, the area of land in which each person can find food becomes smaller, and survival that much more precarious.

The causes of overgrazing

The pastoralists' dependence on milk has serious effects on the savanna. For one thing, it is the main reason for the high proportion of females in their herds. Yet a herd that includes half or more adult females has a phenomenal capacity for reproduction. In a series of two or three good years, the herd can almost double in number. Then when a drought year comes, there are far too many animals on the land and they die. But not before they have ruined the country, laid bare the earth around waterholes and bomas, and killed out the grasses they prefer to eat.

In savannas such as those in Australia or South America, in contrast, large-scale ranchers depend on meat rather than milk to make a living. Unlike the milk-drinking pastoralists, they keep only about twenty-five percent mature cows in their herds. The herds thus cannot increase so fast, and the surplus in any case is sold off at intervals.

The problem in Africa is compounded by the fact that the pastoralists themselves are increasing in numbers. In the old days, tribal warfare, disease, and all the other hazards of life in the bush kept down the numbers of both humans and their livestock. Now they are no longer allowed to fight, and medical care has come to them, if only in a rudimentary way. In addition, veterinarians have provided cures or vaccines for many of the diseases afflicting their livestock.

The end result is that pastoralists such as the Masai are increasing at very nearly the same rate as farmers, doubling in number in about twenty-five years. Since each new family tries to keep the necessary minimum of livestock for milk, meat, and blood, their animals double in number too.

Yet the area of land remains the same. Although the savanna around Borena, for instance, can safely support the

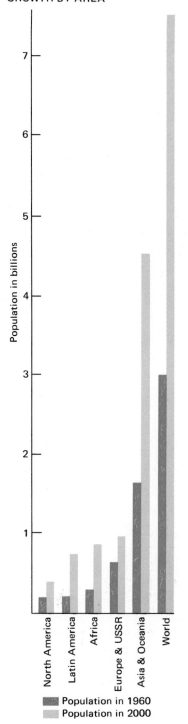

PROJECTED WORLD POPULATION GROWTH BY AREA

Population in billions

North America
Latin America
Africa
Europe & USSR
Asia & Oceania
World

■ Population in 1960
■ Population in 2000

grazing animals of two and a half families per square mile, it immediately becomes overgrazed if just three families try to live on the same area. The effect is scarcely noticeable at first. In a good year the grass still seems vigorous enough. But when a dry year comes, disaster strikes. The huge herds soon weaken and kill desirable species of grass which are replaced by poorer grasses and useless unpalatable shrubs. The large wild animals die out, once-permanent springs dry up, and in the torrential rains, precious soil is washed into gullies and away down rivers. A once-productive savanna becomes a wasteland—and is likely to remain that way permanently unless the land is managed in an entirely different way.

Too many goats and other domestic animals have all but denuded these once productive grazing lands near Lake Baringo in Kenya. As human populations increase, similar scenes of devastation are becoming increasingly common throughout the African plains.

The great conserver

Viewing such a spectacle, as we easily can in many parts of Africa, we think back to the Mwi Valley and the woodlands of the northern Serengeti. How does it happen that these apparently productive grasslands with abundant wildlife remain as uninhabited islands in a sea of populated, often overgrazed country? Although surrounded by aggressive, often hungry pastoral tribes, the Omo and Mwi Valleys remain empty of herdsmen and cattle. Nor do the Masai attempt to push into the northern Serengeti.

No human has ever stopped them from trying. But an insect did—the tsetse fly.

The dreaded tsetse fly is readily distinguished from the common housefly. When at rest, the wings of all species of tsetse flies are conspicuously overlapped, while those of the slightly smaller houseflies spread apart. In addition, tsetse flies hold their mouthparts straight out in front of their heads except when biting, while the mouthparts of houseflies always point downwards.

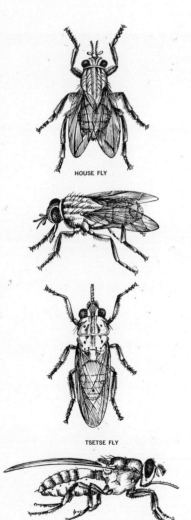

HOUSE FLY

TSETSE FLY

These flies, brown two-winged insects a little larger than house flies, bite us as we move about in the savanna on foot or in our car and when we sit outside the tent in the evening. If we search, we find them buzzing under the fenders of our safari car, which they mistake for some large animal such as a rhinoceros or an elephant. They are stealthy and quiet in their approach. Often we do not realize one is near until a sharp stab of pain behind the knee produces an exclamation and an instinctive slap. We are usually too late, for the fly is quick. In some savannas the flies are so plentiful that life becomes unbearable; one is constantly slapping and cursing.

There are many different kinds of tsetse flies, but all have similar effects. All carry various forms of a group of diseases known as trypanosomiasis, caused by protozoan parasites that live in the blood, more or less as does the parasite that causes malaria. The fly picks up the parasite from the blood of an infected animal which may be a wild animal, a domestic cow, or a human being. The parasite then passes through the fly's gut and into its salivary glands, multiplying in the process. The next time the fly bites an animal, it passes the parasite into the bloodstream of the new host.

When domestic animals, which are not immune to trypanosomiasis, are brought into an area inhabited by tsetse flies, they are bitten at once and infected within days. Before long they sicken and, if not treated, usually die.

The flies can also affect human beings. In the Omo Valley we are bitten only by species of tsetse that carry livestock diseases. In parts of the Serengeti, however, some of the flies also carry the form of trypanosomiasis known as human sleeping sickness. Although the likelihood of contracting the disease is slight, cases do occur occasionally. Murchison Falls Park in Uganda is uninhabited because the flies there can carry sleeping sickness.

In all, tsetse flies infest about a third of the African savannas, and the expenditure of billions of dollars for control has had little permanent effect on the extent of their domain. The flies, in fact, are responsible for the existence of most of the remaining large tracts of uninhabited savannas and the major national parks in Africa. They can be considered a scourge or a savior, depending on one's point of view. Veterinarians and ranchers hate the flies, for they carry disease and death to livestock. They would exterminate

184

them, even if it meant the ultimate ruin of the land. But conservationists, who look with despair on overgrazed and eroded tracts of land, love the tsetse since it keeps men and their cattle away.

It is really no exaggeration to say that it is only because of the tsetse fly that we can today study any tracts of African savanna in their natural state, with all the original species of wild animals still living there in abundance. Otherwise pastoral men would have invaded these areas with their livestock and carved out clan territories.

To kill a fly

Pastoralists with relatively few cattle sometimes manage to live side by side with wild animals without too much difficulty, even in areas infested by tsetse flies. But usually the pressure to get rid of the flies is overwhelming. As a result, in recent years appalling slaughter of wildlife has taken place in several African countries, especially Rhodesia, Zambia, and Uganda, since the wild animals are regarded as reservoirs for the diseases.

The animals were slaughtered by any available means, but even the most efficient hunting methods failed to eliminate all species altogether. Some small, secretive animals, especially the bush duiker, actually were more numerous after the game killers had finished than they were before. And of course they continued to harbor disease and thus to exclude domestic stock. For this reason such areas often had to be abandoned again later—but with most of the wildlife gone and tsetse flies still rampant. In other cases, the method, which is designed to starve the fly out of existence, has seemed to work quite well.

As it turns out, such wholesale slaughter of wildlife was never necessary to control the flies. Tsetses prefer to feed on certain animals above all others—usually species such as wart hogs, elephants, rhinoceroses, buffaloes, or African men that have dark skins. They do not seem to like to feed on animals such as hartebeests or impalas that have bright, glossy skins, and they apparently abhor black-and-white-striped zebras. So it appears that the flies could have been controlled by killing far fewer animals, but by being more selective about what was killed. However, the damage has

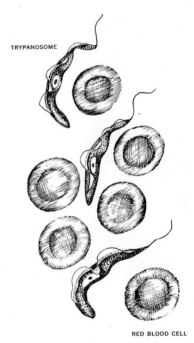

TRYPANOSOME

RED BLOOD CELL

Trypanosomiasis is caused by minute one-celled animals called trypanosomes, shown here among the corpuscles in human blood. The disease spreads when the tsetse fly bites an infected animal and drinks in some of the trypanosomes along with its meal of blood. The disease organisms then multiply in the fly's digestive tract and, as they mature, travel to the fly's salivary glands. When the fly bites a new host, trypanosomes are injected into the animal's blood stream and so are able to infect it with the disease.

LAKE NAKURU NATIONAL PARK

Nestled among rocky hills about 100 miles from Nairobi, the capital of Kenya, is Lake Nakuru, a shallow expanse of water covering about 24 square miles. Although the lake and its immediate surroundings form one of the smaller national parks in Africa, the preserve provides a splendid example of modern Africa's growing awareness of its wildlife heritage, for the park was established primarily as a bird sanctuary. The main attraction in the park is its spectacular concentration of both greater and lesser flamingos. At times, as many as one million of the birds congregate in the lake. Soaring overhead or standing in the water (*left*), the birds are an unforgettable sight for any visitor. Below, left, the birds stand guard over their single eggs, which they lay in simple mud nests. Below, an adult responds to the begging of a nestling. Flamingos are not the only birds that find sanctuary in the park however. In all, nearly four hundred species have been seen in the area, including many kinds of ducks, shorebirds, hawks, vultures, kingfishers, and scores of others.

For some reason, tsetse flies prefer to feed on dark-skinned animals such as elephants (*left*), and avoid others such as striped zebras (*opposite*) and glossy animals such as impalas and hartebeests. Yet in misguided attempts to exterminate this pest, all forms of wildlife—including zebras and impalas—have been killed off over vast areas in Africa.

been done now, and tens of thousands of wild animals have been killed in areas that are still useless for domestic stock. As a result, more and more people are wondering if perhaps the best answer is to forget about keeping domestic animals in fly-infested areas. We still have much to learn about game ranching. Very likely, however, managing and harvesting wild animals will in the long run prove to be a more economical way to use the land in such areas.

The destroyer

So far, in our wanderings through national parks, we have not come across the commonest of large savanna animals, cultivating men. In all, there may be something like 150 million cultivating humans in African savannas—some fifty times as many as there are wildebeests. We saw their work on our way to Murchison Falls National Park from the airport, but then we did not pause to examine their way of life. Now as we fly back to Addis Ababa from the Mwi Valley, we can look out the window of our plane and see how they invade savannas and ultimately destroy them.

It is the end of the dry season, and as we look down on the Ethiopian plateau, we can see countless columns of smoke rising from the savanna-clad foothills. The smoke is not like the widespread clouds that rise from grass fires. Instead it comes from little patches of cleared land where the trunks of trees, shrubs, and dried grass have been piled together and set ablaze. Passing low over one clearing, we can see a man and his wife toiling together, cutting into a new patch of brush to extend their bit of cultivated land, while a pile of cut vegetation burns behind them.

Farther on, as we approach the centers of civilization, the population gradually increases. At first, cleared patches dot the savanna only here and there. In one valley, there may be only twenty cultivated fields, some of them completely new. But in the next valley we see perhaps a hundred small farms, some clotting together in groups of four or five. Possibly these are the farms of the original cultivator, along with those of several sons.

In the next valley, nearly every inch of land seems to be under cultivation. The farms all run together in a continuous area on the slopes and even extend onto steeper hillsides and stony areas. Here the best places have all been used

In sparsely populated areas, farmers clear the natural vegetation from isolated patches of savanna in order to plant cultivated crops. Here a farmer and his family are planting manioc. Within a few years, however, the soil's fertility becomes so depleted that the field must be abandoned and a new clearing made in the savanna.

up, and the descendants of the first colonists have had to make do with less fertile land. Or else they have had to move on to new areas such as the valleys we crossed earlier, and carve out new holdings in untouched savanna.

Almost anywhere we might travel over savanna areas in Africa, or on any other continent, for that matter, the pattern is the same. As human populations grow, the farmers continue to spread into formerly untouched savannas to cultivate their meager crops. And in the process they completely destroy the original vegetation. The native grasses are not merely burned; they are dug up. All trees regarded as useless are cut down and set afire. And the earth that supported both has been dug up, either with cattle-drawn plows or, more often, with hoes or simple sharp-pointed digging sticks.

Once the native vegetation is gone, so too are most of the original savanna animals. Nomadic pastoralists can live pretty well alongside wildlife. They may pass through an area with their herds, but they do not stay forever. Cultivators, on the other hand, will not tolerate wild animals as neighbors. A man who depends on the yield of a few acres of grain can hardly be blamed for wanting to eliminate large herds of buffaloes or zebras from the area. They probably would eat his crops, and so they are hunted or driven away. Smaller antelope are trapped and killed for meat. In inhabited farmland, the only large animal likely to survive in any numbers is the astute baboon. It enjoys men's crops, is too clever to be caught, and is considered inedible by most African farmers.

This spreading pattern of cultivation may be inevitable, for growing human populations must have food. But what seems tragic about the process is its wastefulness. Nowhere is there any attempt to develop the savanna rationally for maximum production. None of the cultivators seem to have any idea of conserving anything—soil, water, vegetation, or wildlife. Instead, a bit of land is cleared and burned, cultivated for a few years until the stored fertility of centuries is gone, then abandoned as the owner moves on to clear— and destroy—another patch of land. Few attempts are made to prevent the soil from being washed down steep slopes in

As human population continues to grow, man's increasing need for food can be met only by cultivating the soil more intensively and more scientifically. In the fertile land of the Kericho district of Kenya, practically every available inch of ground has been planted in cultivated crops.

the torrential savanna storms. Trees are felled for firewood and building poles, but no one plants any trees to replace them. The end result is to create a patch of savanna bare of trees, eroded, and perhaps uninhabitable again by man, while its once abundant wildlife is gone forever.

Obviously people must use the land. But for their own good, the usage should be better controlled and made to provide a more permanent livelihood for the people who live here.

Grain-eaters

Over much of Africa, the main crops grown on savannas are grains of one sort or another, primarily sorghum and millet, as well as corn and a few other grains. Since all the cultivated grains are derived from wild species of grass, it

is only natural that they should prove suitable for cultivation on land that originally supported lush crops of wild grasses. In addition, most of the farms have small patches of bananas and root crops such as yams, manioc, and sweet potatoes. But the staple of the savanna cultivators is invariably grain of some sort, usually mixed with beans, cowpeas, or some other legume that, like grain, can be harvested, dried, and stored for use until the next crop is ripe.

In terms of the total population it can support, cultivation is much more efficient than pastoralism as a way of life. By living on grain and other plant material, cultivating man becomes a primary user of vegetation, while the pastoralist is a secondary user who first allows the vegetation to pass through his animals. Just as the savanna supports a greater biomass of herbivores than carnivores among wild animals, it can sustain more grain-eaters than meat-eaters.

A little simple arithmetic can prove this point. In the

Using only a primitive ox-drawn plow, a farmer in the Simyen mountains in northern Ethiopia does his best to scratch a living from barren rocky soil. Trying to grow unimproved varieties of grain on such poor soil in an area of low rainfall, he is likely to get so meager a yield from his crops that he can attain only a subsistence level of existence.

Millet, one of the basic crops grown by African farmers, produces abundant yields of nutritious grain. Sorghum, corn, beans, cowpeas, and root crops such as manioc and yams also are important staples in the African's diet. But to keep a growing population fed, improved varieties of all these plants must be developed and farming methods must be made more efficient.

area of southern Ethiopia that we considered earlier, we saw that two and a half families of pastoralists, or twenty people, could subsist comfortably on their livestock on one square mile of savanna. In the same area, with an annual rainfall of about thirty inches, cultivators using primitive tools, no fertilizers, and only the local unimproved varieties of grain could grow an average crop of one thousand pounds per acre. Since a family of eight, half of them children under fourteen, needs about ten pounds of grain a day to subsist, their annual need would thus be provided by the yield of about three and a half acres of land.

Of course they could not live on just this minimum amount of land. For every acre actually under cultivation in any year, another three acres must lie fallow so that its fertility can be replenished. In addition, about half the land in the area cannot be cultivated at all because of steep stony slopes or swampy places. Even so, this works out to a total potential population in the area of 21 families, or 168 people, per square mile—nearly eight and a half times the total of 20 people who could subsist here by pastoralism alone! And at that, in this example, about seven-eighths of the land in any year would still be available for keeping livestock!

Thus it seems inevitable that wherever there is enough rain to support agriculture—at least twenty-five inches or so per year—pastoralists will ultimately have to turn to cultivation for their livelihoods in savannas. And if the native farmers took better care of the soil, used fertilizer, and planted superior varieties of grains, even greater numbers of people would be able to live on the land. A great deal of money would have to be spent on roads, water supplies, schools, medical facilities, and all the other needs of growing populations. In the end, it is quite possible that certain savannas could support human populations as great as 670 to 1000 people per square mile—denser than in a developed industrial country such as Great Britain or Holland!

If we were to convert human beings and their livestock into standing crop biomass, as we did with the wild animals at Serengeti, we would find that this high figure about equals the maximum—250,000 pounds per square mile—of wild animals that can be supported on similar savanna. At the rate that human populations are growing, the day when such densities are reached may not be far away.

Manioc, or cassava, is a major food crop throughout the tropics. The plant is cultivated for the sake of its large underground tubers, which may be as much as three feet long and weigh ten pounds each. The meal prepared from the tubers, though rich in starch, is poor in many nutrients.

Large-scale farmers

In other savannas such as those of South America or Australia, most of the inhabitants are large-scale ranchers or farmers rather than subsistence cultivators. Instead of using digging sticks or ox-drawn plows, they use expensive modern machinery to clear and cultivate huge tracts of land. But their effects on the habitat are much the same.

Smaller birds and mammals may have a better chance of survival on large farms and ranches than in areas densely populated with small-scale farms. When peasant farmers cut down the trees, they destroy the homes of hornbills, glossy starlings, bush babies, squirrels, and many other savanna creatures. Ranchers and large-scale farmers do not clear steep slopes or small patches in river valleys where they cannot use machinery. Since their cultivated fields are separated by large tracts of rough grazing land, many of the small birds and mammals that lived in the original savanna can survive.

For large animals, however, the result is always the same: cultivation spells doom. No farmer will permit large herds of buffaloes or zebras near his cultivated grain fields. Nor will he allow them to compete with the cattle on his grazing land. And he looks askance at the presence of

Cultivation spells doom for many savanna animals. Predators are destroyed or driven off, as are large grazers that would compete with domestic stock for forage. Baboons, however, are so intelligent and adaptable that they manage to thrive even on farms and near villages.

elephants and giraffes because of their tendency to damage or destroy water supplies and fences. So he usually drives off or destroys large numbers of these animals.

Leopards often survive on large farms, and are even valued because of their habit of killing baboons, pigs, and porcupines. But the farmers usually destroy other predators such as lions and hyenas which might attack their cattle. As a result, smaller antelope such as duikers, impalas, and bushbucks often survive in quite good numbers since they are freed of the menace of their natural enemies. The farmers may regard them as a nuisance, but usually consider them too much trouble to shoot. In some cases, they even welcome the small grazers because of their beauty or the sport they provide.

One way in which the rancher differs from his small-scale counterpart is in his attitude toward fire. The rancher usually makes strenuous efforts to prevent fires, except as a deliberate tool for suppressing brush. With the annual contrast between black burned ground and lush new growth avoided, the resident population of small animals is probably more stable and better able to survive the dry season. Pastoralists, honey hunters, and small-scale farmers, in contrast, usually set off the annual holocaust with no thought whatsoever for the future.

On large-scale farms, brushy areas are often left uncleared and large tracts are left in rough grazing lands. As a result, bushbucks and other small antelope continue to prosper, largely because the farmers kill off the leopards and other predators that might attack their cattle.

What will happen to savannas?

If we were to repeat the journey with which we began this excursion into the savanna, this time traveling from uninhabited plains back to the town and airport, we would have to regard the small farms we pass from a different point of view. If we pause to reflect, we are certain to realize that they are the most potent force that has ever been unleashed to change the conditions of life on the African plains.

Africa, like the rest of the world, is undergoing a population explosion. At present, 150 million or more cultivators live on African savannas, and their numbers are likely to double within twenty-five years. Each year a quarter of a million new families must find new land to cultivate. Even infestations of tsetse flies do not always stop the onrush of cultivators, who often keep few cattle. Where there is no natural savanna, the cultivators destroy the forests and create derived savannas.

The basic problem is that the farmers are untrained and, of necessity, concerned only with their immediate survival. Their primitive methods of cultivation are basically destructive, not only to the vast and varied assemblage of savanna wildlife, but to the land itself. As soil erosion accelerates, as useless brush takes over, and as other symptoms of a degenerating landscape appear, the farmers will have to abandon their now worthless fields and move on to new areas—if they can find any.

The destruction is not deliberate. The farmers, like other inhabitants of the savanna, are trying to survive in the only ways known to them. Plainly, however, if we are to prevent total ruination of the few remaining tracts of unspoiled natural savanna and achieve greater productivity for human beings in already populated areas, we must teach them to use the land more wisely and efficiently. But time is running out. The changes must come soon.

Silhouetted against an evening sky, a lone gazelle contemplates the savanna landscape. Can we save enough of this precious resource in its natural state so that future generations will be able to marvel at the incredibly varied life of the African plains?

Appendix

National Parks of the African Plains

In Africa as elsewhere in the world, people are becoming increasingly aware of their wildlife heritage. More and more, they are coming to realize that the dwindling remnants of the vast herds that once roamed the African plains are national treasures that must be protected and preserved. These priceless resources must be conserved not only for the benefit of present-day Africans but also for the enjoyment of future generations of Africans and of people from all over the world who come to Africa for a glimpse of Eden. In an effort to preserve the natural savanna habitat and its wildlife populations, the nations of Africa have set aside tracts of land, some of them of great size.

These reservations vary in name. Some are true national parks, while others are called game reserves, game preserves, conservation areas, wildlife reserves, and sanctuaries. They also differ greatly in the amount of protection given to the wildlife, in their hunting restrictions, in the degree to which human disturbance of the habitat is allowed, in types and amount of supervision, and in the kinds of visitor accommodations that are provided. Some of the parks exist in name only. Though formally designated as sanctuaries, they have yet to be staffed or developed for the convenience of visitors.

In all cases, however, the ultimate objective is the same: to prevent destruction of the land and its unique wildlife. People all over the world can be grateful to the nations of Africa for taking steps to preserve these matchless treasures. On the following pages are descriptions of the attractions at some of the outstanding savanna parks and preserves of Africa.

ETHIOPIA

Awash National Park
Located at the edge of the Rift Valley about 135 miles east of the capital city of Addis Ababa, this 319-square-mile park consists mainly of arid plains. While vegetation is sparse, it becomes more abundant in the Awash River Valley. A variety of plains animals live in the park, including both greater and lesser kudus, Soemmering's gazelles, and numbers of the rare Beisa oryx. A campsite and a hotel are available for visitors.

SOEMMERING'S GAZELLE

Omo National Park

Although officially designated a national park, this area has yet to be developed for visitors. Presently accessible only by air from Jimma, the 1200-square-mile park in the southwestern corner of Ethiopia encompasses a broad U-shaped river valley. Abundant wildlife, including many plains animals, make the area worthy of preservation. At present no accommodations are provided, but visitors are permitted to use an unoccupied warden's house.

Rift Valley Lakes National Park

Also proclaimed but undeveloped as a national park, this 335-square-mile area is situated 150 miles south of Addis Ababa on the Ethiopia-Kenya highway, with headquarters at Neghelie. The prime attractions at the park are two lakes, Shala and Abiata, which are important stopovers for migrating waterfowl. In January and February, thousands of ducks and geese of many species rest in the lakes. Pelicans, flamingos, and storks also are abundant and nest on islands in the lakes. Lakeside campsites are available, and there are small hotels on nearby roads.

KENYA

Aberdare National Park

This 293-square-mile mountain park is in Kenya's Central Highlands about 13 miles from the town of Nyeri. Although not strictly a plains park, it is included here because it is the home of the world-renowned Treetops Hotel. The building, perched on stiltlike pilings, towers above an active waterhole and artificial salt lick. From the hotel, guests can comfortably and at close range observe such plains species as elephants, rhinos, Cape buffaloes, waterbucks, Bohor reedbucks, and many other mammals, including the giant forest hog. In addition to Treetops, several campsites are provided in the park, and other hotel accommodations are available in Nyeri.

Amboseli Masai Game Reserve

Located on the Tanzania border about 150 miles south of Nairobi, this 1259-square-mile reserve can be reached via the Nairobi-Mombasa highway. The park, with the snow-covered peak of Mount Kilimanjaro as a backdrop, is a picturesque mixture of thorn scrub savanna, grassland, acacia woodland, marshes, and a dry lake bed. More than eighty species of mammals live in the reserve, including the black rhinoceros, the gerenuk, the fringe-eared oryx, the golden jackal, and the noc-

GOLDEN JACKAL

204

turnal aardwolf. The three big cats—the lion, the leopard, and the cheetah—all are easily observed here, as are many kinds of birds, including the Masai ostrich, three species of sand grouse, and the otherwise rare Taveta golden weaver. Several lodges, tent camps, and campsites are located within the reserve.

Lake Nakuru National Park
Primarily a bird sanctuary, this small park comprises twenty-four-square-mile Lake Nakuru and the surrounding shoreline, woodlands, grasslands, and scrub. The prime attraction is the hordes of flamingos—estimated at over a million—that sometimes congregate on the lake, but the park also provides sanctuary for great numbers of other shore and water birds such as ducks, geese, pelicans, herons, gulls, terns, plovers, and sandpipers. Cape buffaloes, a small herd of hippos, and many other mammals also live in or regularly visit the park. Overnight accommodations are available in the nearby town of Nakuru.

Mara Masai Game Reserve
Although smaller and less well known than Tanzania's Serengeti National Park, which lies just across the international border and adjoins Mara Masai, this 550-square-mile reserve is impressive in every way. The rolling landscape includes open woodland savanna, thorn-scrub savanna, acacia woodlands, and a network of forest-bordered streams. The vast grazing herds include oribis, wildebeests, hartebeests, Grant's gazelles, giraffes, and zebras. The reserve is especially famous for its lion population, its large herds of topis, and the presence of the handsome but elusive roan antelope. Bird life is unbelievably varied. No less than fifty-three species of birds of prey have been recorded here, including the rare African fishing owl. For the convenience of visitors, there are many miles of dirt roads for viewing animals. Accommodations are available at a few campsites and the luxurious Keekorok Lodge.

Meru National Park
This magnificent 366-square-mile tract, located northeast of Mount Kenya, includes a great variety of habitats: rolling grasslands, acacia savanna, doum palm savanna, bush savanna, and, at the northern end of the park, even a rain forest. Although much of the park is accessible by car or motorboat, there is also a large wilderness area where the visitor must travel on foot with a ranger guide and safari gear. The park is noted for its lions—the famous lioness Elsa was studied here by Joy Adamson —but also boasts white rhinos (introduced from South Africa), rarities such as the lesser kudu and Beisa oryx, and a rich variety

AARDWOLF

of birds, including the elusive Peters' finfoot. Two lodges and two camps are available for tourists.

Nairobi National Park
Located only four miles from the center of Nairobi, this forty-four-square-mile preserve is the gem among Kenya's parks. Though small, it boasts a superb variety of wildlife. Ranging over the open plains are giraffes, hartebeests, impalas, Grant's gazelles, Thomson's gazelles, elands, zebras, lions, baboons, and a wealth of other mammals. Birds are equally varied: over 450 species have been seen here, ranging in size from ostriches to tiny white-eyes. A zoo without bars and an aviary without fences, the park is an ideal place to begin—or end—a journey through East Africa.

Tsavo National Park
With an area of 8024 square miles, this is East Africa's largest park. Habitats in this vast arid tract include mountain forest, palm thickets, open plains, scrub savanna, and semidesert scrub. The park is noted for its elephant watering hole at the base of the Mudanda Rock and for the crystal clear Mzima Springs. Cape buffaloes, waterbucks, impalas, gerenuks, elands, and other herbivores can be seen, as well as their attendant predators. The fantastic bird life includes twenty-four species of shrikes and at least sixty-six kinds of sparrows, weavers, and other finches, plus an abundance of parrots, rollers, barbets, and starlings. Although some parts of the park are roadless and uninhabited by man, the visitor is well provided for. There are 500 miles of roads for viewing animals, two lodges with complete accommodations, two other lodges where food must be brought in, and a few campsites.

REPUBLIC OF SOUTH AFRICA

Kalahari Gemsbok National Park
This 3456-square-mile park in northwestern South Africa adjoins the similar but larger Kalahari Gemsbok Game Reserve in Botswana. Both areas are administered by South African personnel. The semidesert landscape is largely uninhabited, although nomadic bushmen move through it periodically. Even so, a variety of plains animals roam the sparse scrubby grasslands, including feral camels, gemsboks, springboks, elands, hartebeests, wildebeests, and lions. Among the more prominent birds are sociable weavers. The park is open year-round, but is extremely hot in December and January. Lodgings are available at Twee Riverien and Mata-Mata.

GEMSBOK

Kruger National Park

Kruger is the oldest and one of Africa's largest and best-known national parks. Located in northeastern South Africa, its 7340 square miles include scenic hill country, scrubby woodlands, parklike savannas, and open grassland. Vast numbers of animals live here: an estimated 2000 elephants, 13,000 zebras, and 17 species of antelope, including 180,000 impalas. There are also about 1000 lions, 600 to 700 leopards, and 250 cheetahs. The park is a true tourist mecca, attracting almost 300,000 visitors each year. Tourist facilities are comfortable and plentiful.

Mountain Zebra National Park

This small park, nineteen square miles in area, was established specifically to protect the rare mountain zebra, a small race of the common, or Burchell's, zebra. However, its expanses of flat grasslands, open acacia woodlands, and surrounding hills also provide sanctuary for elands, white-tailed wildebeests, gemsboks, blesboks, ostriches, and a variety of other animals. Campsites are available. About 150 miles to the south is another small park, Addo Elephant National Park, which was created to protect a small herd of diminutive Cape elephants. Similar in purpose is Bontebok National Park, whose prize is a growing herd of bonteboks, once the rarest antelope in the world. From a low of 17 survivors, the present population numbers several hundred.

RHODESIA

VERREAUX'S EAGLE

Rhodes Matopos National Park

Located just south of Bulawayo, this 200-square-mile park is primarily an archeological site, but many plains animals can be seen on the woodland savanna and in a fenced game park. The exceptionally rich bird life includes an astonishing concentration of Verreaux's eagles.

Victoria Falls National Park

The famous falls on the Zambesi River are the central attraction of this park in western Rhodesia. Except for the heavily forested river valley, much of the terrain is arid plains. A good variety of grazers are to be seen here, including notable numbers of sable antelope, while the river attracts many kinds of birds such as cormorants, herons, and shorebirds. Accommodations include lodges and campsites.

Wankie National Park

This large park is fifty miles south of Victoria Falls, in southwestern Rhodesia. Its 5540 square miles of arid scrublands and bush are noted for their concentrations of plains wildlife, including sable antelope, roan antelope, sassaby, and even a few gemsboks. A rest camp is provided, and roads through the park afford excellent opportunities for viewing game.

RWANDA

Kagera National Park
This 970-square-mile park in northeastern Rwanda borders on Tanzania and Uganda. The terrain consists of a series of broad valleys with grasslands and acacia savannas, as well as some lakes and extensive marshes. Wildlife is similar to that in nearby Queen Elizabeth National Park in Uganda. There is a guest house at Gabiro.

SUDAN

DOUM PALM

Dinder National Park
This magnificent 2470-square-mile park about 300 miles southeast of Khartoum consists mainly of savanna woodland, with groves of doum palms and forests of acacias, tamarinds, and fig trees along watercourses. Among the grazers to be seen here are giraffes, tora hartebeests, greater kudus, waterbucks, oribis, and several gazelles, including the large Soemmering's gazelle. Lions, leopards, and other predators also are present, while the varied birdlife includes such savanna species as ostriches, bustards, francolins, and quails. A main road crosses the park, and rougher tracks lead to viewing areas. A rest camp, three campsites, and several viewing blinds are provided for visitors.

Nimule National Park
Although so far undeveloped and presently difficult of access, this 96-square-mile preserve has great potential as a tourist attraction. The park is located on the Nile River at the Uganda border in extreme southern Sudan. It consists mainly of river plains and smaller tributary valleys, with extensive areas of bush and savanna grasslands. Some of the more conspicuous herbivores are white rhinoceroses, elephants, and Cape buffaloes.

Southern National Park
This vast, undeveloped 6176-square-mile area is about 570 miles southwest of Khartoum. Generally uninhabited and trackless, it consists mostly of flat arid bush country. The large population

of plains wildlife includes elephants, giraffes, and white rhinos and features giant elands, roan antelopes, and lelwel hartebeests. At present, however, the park is virtually inaccessible, has no accommodations for visitors, and is in a politically disturbed area.

TANZANIA

Lake Manyara National Park

The central feature of this 123-square-mile park is the shallow expanse of Lake Manyara, bordered on the north by the steep escarpment of the Rift Valley and on the south by open plains. The marshes, forests, acacia woodlands, and scrubby areas of the park abound with tree-climbing lions, elephants, buffaloes, and rhinos. The tiny dwarf mongoose inhabits termite mounds along the main road. Birdlife includes waterfowl, shorebirds, flamingos, pelicans, herons, kingfishers, cuckoos, bee eaters, hornbills, barbets, honey guides, and many more. Besides campsites, there is a lodge, Lake Manyara Hotel, commanding a spectacular view of lake and forests.

Ngorongoro Crater Conservation Area

Formerly a part of Serengeti National Park, this 2500-square-mile tract is now administered separately. The preserve centers on the 9-mile-wide, 2000-foot-deep crater of an extinct volcano. A veritable bowlful of wildlife, the crater is populated with large numbers of elephants, rhinos, buffaloes, wildebeests, zebras, gazelles, hyenas, jackals, bat-eared foxes, and elands. Bush duikers and giant forest hogs lurk on the wooded slopes of the crater's rim, while great flocks of waterbirds congregate about lakes on the crater's floor. The area is also known for the Masai tribesmen who live here and tend herds of cattle. The only accommodation, Ngorongoro Lodge, is perched on the crater's rim.

Ruaha National Park

Tanzania's second largest park, at 4600 square miles, is far less known and visited than Serengeti. Only partially developed and still completely unspoiled, it is an expanse of plateau highlands in south-central Tanzania, with extensive brachystegia and acacia woodlands, grasslands, and rocky cliffs and outcrops. In the dry season, many plains animals congregate around the two rivers that cross the park, the Ruaha and the Njombe. The park boasts both greater and lesser kudus, roan and sable antelopes, and the largest elephant herd in Tanzania. Crocodiles are common along the Ruaha River, and birds are plentiful everywhere. Visitor facilities include campsites, tree houses, and photography blinds.

BAT-EARED FOX

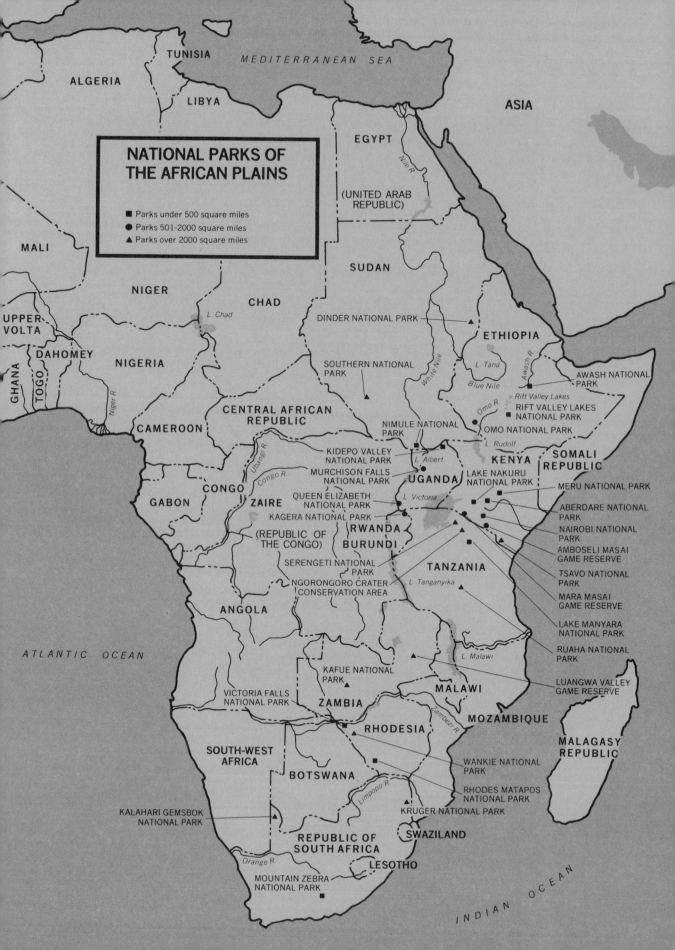

NATIONAL PARKS OF THE AFRICAN PLAINS

■ Parks under 500 square miles
● Parks 501-2000 square miles
▲ Parks over 2000 square miles

MEDITERRANEAN SEA

TUNISIA

ALGERIA

LIBYA

ASIA

EGYPT
(UNITED ARAB
REPUBLIC)

Nile R.

MALI

NIGER

CHAD

L. Chad

SUDAN

UPPER-
VOLTA

DINDER NATIONAL PARK

ETHIOPIA

L. Tana

Awash R.

GHANA
TOGO
DAHOMEY

NIGERIA

SOUTHERN NATIONAL
PARK

White Nile

Blue Nile

AWASH NATIONAL
PARK

Omo R.

Rift Valley Lakes

RIFT VALLEY LAKES
NATIONAL PARK

CAMEROON

CENTRAL AFRICAN
REPUBLIC

NIMULE NATIONAL
PARK

OMO NATIONAL PARK

L. Rudolf

Niger R.

Ubangi R.

KIDEPO VALLEY
NATIONAL PARK

L. Albert

KENYA

SOMALI
REPUBLIC

GABON

CONGO

ZAIRE

Congo R.

MURCHISON FALLS
NATIONAL PARK

UGANDA

LAKE NAKURU
NATIONAL PARK

MERU NATIONAL PARK

QUEEN ELIZABETH
NATIONAL PARK

L. Victoria

ABERDARE NATIONAL
PARK

(REPUBLIC OF
THE CONGO)

KAGERA NATIONAL PARK

RWANDA
BURUNDI

NAIROBI NATIONAL
PARK

AMBOSELI MASAI
GAME RESERVE

SERENGETI NATIONAL
PARK

TANZANIA

TSAVO NATIONAL
PARK

ANGOLA

NGORONGORO CRATER
CONSERVATION AREA

L. Tanganyika

MARA MASAI
GAME RESERVE

LAKE MANYARA
NATIONAL PARK

ATLANTIC OCEAN

RUAHA NATIONAL
PARK

L. Malawi

LUANGWA VALLEY
GAME RESERVE

KAFUE NATIONAL
PARK

MALAWI

VICTORIA FALLS
NATIONAL PARK

ZAMBIA

MOZAMBIQUE

SOUTH-WEST
AFRICA

Zambezi R.

RHODESIA

MALAGASY
REPUBLIC

BOTSWANA

WANKIE NATIONAL
PARK

RHODES MATAPOS
NATIONAL PARK

KALAHARI GEMSBOK
NATIONAL PARK

Limpopo R.

KRUGER NATIONAL PARK

SWAZILAND

REPUBLIC OF
SOUTH AFRICA

Orange R.

LESOTHO

INDIAN OCEAN

MOUNTAIN ZEBRA
NATIONAL PARK

Serengeti National Park
This 5600-square-mile park in northwestern Tanzania is world renowned for its spectacular concentrations of game animals, and their regular migrations across the park. More than 2,000,000 large herbivores live here, including 750,000 wildebeests, over 1 million Thomson's gazelles, and vast numbers of zebras, Grant's gazelles, giraffes, and other grazers. The park is also noted for its many prides of lions and easily observed leopards and cheetahs. Although most of the park is typical savanna grassland, there are also acacia and savanna woodlands, forested river edges, and even a few marshes and lakes. In addition to campsites, the park has a comfortable lodge at Seronera.

UGANDA

Kidepo Valley National Park
This relatively remote and undeveloped 486-square-mile park is in a spectacularly scenic mountain area in northern Uganda along the Sudan border. The drier eastern part of the park is arid savanna, while the wetter (and better developed) south-western part of the park is an area of tall-grass savanna. Here the visitor can see hartebeests, elands, zebras, oribis, roan antelopes, klipspringers, Kirk's dik-diks, greater and lesser kudus, elephants, Cape buffaloes, black rhinos, and all the major predators. Bird attractions include a rich variety of birds of prey, Abyssinian ground hornbills, and standard-winged nightjars. There are visitors' lodges at Apoka, on the park's southern boundary, and an airstrip at nearby Kilabe.

STANDARD-WINGED NIGHTJAR

Murchison Falls National Park
Uganda's largest park encompasses 1557 square miles of rolling savanna grasslands, acacia woodlands, one forest inhabited by chimpanzees, and extensive papyrus beds along the Victoria Nile, which flows across the park. The most famous landmark is the spectacular cascade of Murchison Falls flowing through a narrow gorge, while the most popular tourist attraction is a boat trip along the river below the falls. Cruising along the river, the visitor has a fine opportunity to observe rhinos, waterbucks, and crocodiles on the banks; hippos in the water; and storks, pelicans, herons, cormorants, kingfishers, terns, and skimmers overhead. On the grasslands are large numbers of elephants, antelope, oribis, kobs, lions, leopards, and many other animals. The park has two lodges, Paraa and Chobe, as well as campsites and an airstrip.

Queen Elizabeth National Park

Lying between Lake George and Lake Edward on the western border of Uganda, this 767-square-mile park overlooks the spectacular Ruwenzori Range, the "Mountains of the Moon." The mixture of open grasslands, euphorbia-dotted savannas, tropical forests, swamps, and waterways results in richly varied wildlife, such as elephants, Cape buffaloes, topis, kobs, waterbucks, and bushbucks. The park also boasts six species of monkeys but is more famous for its birdlife, including the saddle-billed stork and the rare whale-headed stork. Visitors can stay at Mweya Lodge or at campsites in the park.

ZAMBIA

Kafue National Park

This well-managed 8492-square-mile park straddling the Kafue River includes semidesert woodlands, open scrub woodlands, and, in the north, broad, rich savanna grasslands. The larger herbivores and their attendant predators all are present, but the park is especially notable for its variety of antelope. Besides the commoner species, Kafue boasts roan and sable antelope, red lechwes, sitatungas, oribis, blue duikers, gray duikers, steinboks, and Sharpe's grysboks. The park, open from July to December, is well equipped with a hotel at Ngoma, several rest camps, 500 miles of viewing roads, and an airstrip.

Luangwa Valley Game Reserve

This is one of several game reserves in Zambia incorporating game management areas in which controlled hunting is permitted. The 4760-square-mile tract is also the site of an experiment in managing wild game for food production. Many plains animals are present, including the rare Cookson's hartebeest. The reserve, open from June to October, has rest camps, hotel-type camps, and game-watching areas. Other Zambian game reserves are 1144-square-mile Mweru Marsh; 738-square-mile Sumbu, on the shore of Lake Tanganyika; and smaller, less developed reserves at Kasanka, Lunga, and Lusenga.

WHALE-HEADED STORK

212

Planning a Safari Vacation

In these days of modern jet travel, more and more people are journeying to Africa each year to see at first hand the wildlife of the plains. Planning such a trip can involve the simple matter of phoning a travel agent or the more complicated task of making all the arrangements yourself. By employing the services of a travel agent, you can profit from the expertise of people who know both Africa and the travel business better than you do. If you choose to arrange your own trip, however, you will have the advantage of going when you want, where you want, and with companions of your own choosing.

For most people, the wisest course is to go on a prearranged group tour. Wildlife safaris are now conducted by several reputable conservation organizations including the National Audubon Society, the Massachusetts Audubon Society, the National Wildlife Federation, and the Sierra Club. In addition, group safaris are offered by a number of experienced and reliable commercial tour operators. In many cases, the commercial tours have experienced naturalists as leaders.

Prearranged tours vary considerably in price, depending on such things as the point of departure, the size of the group, the type of ground transportation provided in Africa, the number and duration of stops, the qualifications of the tour guides, and the kind of accommodations used for overnight stops. Some of the so-called "bargain" safaris race around the famous high spots. Other more leisurely tours visit carefully selected parks and preserves by minibus or land rover, while still other groups hop from park to park by light aircraft. Finally there are camping safaris which avoid hotels and lodges altogether and make all overnight stops in tented camps.

With such a variety of trips to choose from, it is obviously advisable to shop around and get literature from as many tour sponsors as possible. To find the tour that is best suited to your interests, you will want to know how many others will be in your party, how many persons there will be per guide and per vehicle, what kind of accommodations are offered, what the age profile of the group will be, what special interests will be catered to, and so forth. Economy tours, for example, often travel with nine persons to a three-seat minibus. The result is discomfort for all—and poor visibility for the unfortunates in the middle seats.

For watching and photographing game, a window seat for each passenger is ideal. Yet overlooking a seemingly minor detail like this can significantly detract from your enjoyment of the trip.

If you should decide to make all your own arrangements, you should be aware of the disadvantages as well as the advantages. Driving on bumpy, dusty, and sometimes muddy African roads, for instance, is not always a pleasure. Automobile services are often widely scattered and sometimes simply unobtainable. At all the more popular national parks, reservations for accommodations must be made, often months in advance. You must make all your own arrangements for permits, fees, and fares. Lack of an experienced guide (native guides are remarkably keen-eyed game spotters) may deprive you of many sightings, or at least of the information a guide would have provided. Finally, while you can cut expenses by camping instead of staying at lodges or hotels, your airfare is likely to cost more than if you were traveling with a group.

Thus, even if you are planning your own trip, it is advisable to consult one of the many travel agencies in Nairobi, Johannesburg, Kampala, and other major cities. They can make many of your essential prior arrangements and reservations, help with your schedule, and provide transportation, safari gear, and guides if desired.

When to go

In a region as extensive as the plains areas of Africa, the climate varies considerably. East Africa, for instance, is equatorial, while much of Sudan and South-West Africa is arid desert. South African climates, in turn, range from subtropical to temperate. Throughout the entire area, however, elevation is more important than latitude. The coast of Kenya, for example, steams under lowland tropical heat. Inland, however, are temperate

highlands, while the slopes of Mount Kilimanjaro are alpine, and the crests of Mount Kilimanjaro and Mount Kenya—almost on the equator—are clothed in perpetual snow.

Fortunately, most of the savanna national parks are in the highlands where the climate is pleasant, with warm days and cool nights. In East Africa there are four seasons. January and February are the dry season, and the warmest time of the year. In March the "long rains" arrive, inaugurating the growing season and the greening of the plains. June, July, and August bring cool, cloudy days with some rain, followed by a brief second dry season that lasts until the "short rains" come from late October until mid-December. Here the best game viewing probably is in January and February, although it is good in all months except during the "short rains" from October to December. Parks, however, are open year-round.

In Rhodesia and South Africa, on the other hand, there are basically two seasons, a rainy summer from late November through April and a dry winter from May to October. In South Africa, the best months for viewing game are August, September, and October, when the plains are dry and wildlife concentrates at rivers and waterholes. In Rhodesia the best season is from July to October, when there is almost no rain at all. Parks in Rhodesia are closed to visitors from November until June, and in South Africa they are closed from December until April, although part of Kruger National Park is open year-round. Botswana is extremely hot in October and November, with temperatures frequently over 100 degrees Fahrenheit.

What to take

Since space is limited in touring vehicles, most tour sponsors request that you limit luggage to one all-purpose suitcase, one smaller overnight bag, and, if desired, a shoulder-slung gadget

bag for binoculars, camera, film, and field guides. If you organize your own trip, of course, you can set your own limits on luggage. In these days of wrinkle-free clothing and drip-dry fabrics, however, traveling light is a practical reality.

For the most part, ordinary lightweight summer clothing is entirely adequate for a visit to the African plains. Do take rain gear, however, and remember that at higher elevations, day-time temperatures in the eighties often drop below sixty at night, so that sweaters, warm jackets, or topcoats will be welcome additions to your wardrobe for evening wear.

Although many European Africans wear walking shorts or skirts in the field, most Americans—both men and women—will feel most comfortable in khaki or chino slacks. Besides discouraging insect bites, they will protect you from scratches from thorny acacias and sharp-edged sedges. For all clothing, neutral earth tones are better than bright colors.

Also recommended are the so-called "bush shirts" or slightly heavier "bush jackets" with four capacious pockets. These are available through many American sportsmen's outfitters, but are usually less expensive in Africa. Bush shirts are ideal for travelers with camera equipment and other gadgets since the pockets provide handy storage compartments for film, lenses, notebooks, field guides, and so on.

A broad-brimmed hat is useful, and good-quality sunglasses are essential. Comfortable shoes also are desirable, although you will do little walking: in most parks it is forbidden to alight from your vehicle in game-viewing areas. Finally, you will probably want to take along one or two more formal outfits for traveling, for use on European or other stopovers, and for dinners at the more formal lodges. Jackets and slacks for the men and drip-dry dresses for the ladies are entirely adequate, however; the evenings of the black tie dinner in the jungle camp are gone forever.

As for optical equipment, it is not necessary to carry an arsenal of gadgets to enjoy Africa. In fact, the traveler with a simple camera and compact binoculars often seems to see the most. Your needs, however, will depend entirely on your own interests and degree of expertise.

If you are at all serious about studying bird and animal life, binoculars are essential. The best are sturdy, center focus, coated lens binoculars of at least seven power. For watching birds, eight, ten, or even twelve power are desirable. For viewing living birds and animals at even closer range, some sort of telescope can be useful, although you may frequently find it difficult or even impossible to set up the tripod, especially on commercial tours. Needless to add, dust covers are recommended for all exposed lenses since dust is pervasive on all African roads.

The choice of cameras is up to the individual, depending on his goals, his skills, and the amount of time available for photography. Since it is possible to approach most plains animals quite closely in vehicles, inexpensive snapshot cameras with all-purpose lenses are adequate for many visitors. If photography is your primary objective, however, bring your arsenal. For scenery, a wide-angle lens is ideal. For people and average close-ups, use your normal lens. For game and birds, somewhat longer lenses are useful, although extremely long telephoto lenses are unnecessary, since most game can be approached quite closely.

Odds and ends

A small flashlight is likely to prove useful, especially if you stay in any of the tented camps, where the electricity is usually turned off at bedtime. Note, too, that electric razors and other American-made appliances may not operate on the local current unless you equip yourself with a converter.

There is no need to overload yourself with ordinary toiletries, since they are readily available everywhere, as are insect repellants and film for your camera. If you depend on eyeglasses, however, bring along a spare pair in case of breakage. Also bring a supply of any special prescription medicines you may require.

International health requirements call for immunization against smallpox and yellow fever. Your physician may also recommend gamma-globulin, antitetanus, and possibly typhoid-paratyphoid and cholera shots.

As for potential dangers, you will have little to fear if you obey regulations and follow the instructions of your guides. Even the biggest game animals can be safely viewed from inside a vehicle. Although there are several poisonous snakes in Africa, the average visitor is not likely ever to encounter one. And except for the tsetse fly, biting insects are virtually absent in the highlands.

Finally, remember that you are a guest in a foreign country. If you treat the people with courtesy and respect, you will find them friendly, cooperative, and anxious to help you make your safari a memorable experience.

Africa's Endangered Wildlife

To a visitor touring the great national parks and preserves of the African plains, the wildlife may seem so incredibly varied and abundant that he may find it difficult to believe that some species are—or were until recently—in real danger of extinction. Yet even the great herds of wildebeests and zebras in Serengeti National Park, the elephants of Tsavo National Park, and the menagerie of antelope at Kruger National Park are little more than remnants of the vast assemblages of animals that once populated the plains.

Many forces contributed to the startling decimation of African wildlife that has taken place over the past century or so. Some of the animals fell victim to imported diseases, such as the deadly rinderpest that European settlers brought with their domestic livestock. Before it was brought under control, the disease all but wiped out several native game species. Farmers, both large and small, also have caused problems for wildlife by damaging the native habitat. Even land that has not been cleared to plant crops is often so badly overgrazed by domestic stock that little forage is left for wild animals.

The greatest destruction of African wildlife, however, has been by hunters. Farmers shoot trespassing animals that might compete

SOMALI WILD ASS
This rare subspecies of the African wild ass once was plentiful on arid grasslands of the Somali Republic and Ethiopia. Now the combined effects of hunting and competition with domestic animals for forage have reduced the population to a few hundred animals in widely scattered herds. Only strict protection and the establishment of game sanctuaries can save it from extinction.

BONTEBOK
One of the rarest of antelope, the bontebok once was nearly exterminated by unrestricted hunting and settlement of its natural range in the Cape Province of the Republic of South Africa. Establishment of Bontebok National Park and protection of several herds on private land, however, have resulted in an increase in numbers to a present population of several hundred of this brown and white antelope.

with their domestic stock for food. Sportsmen from all over the world come to Africa to hunt for trophies. And protein-starved Africans continue to hunt animals for food, even if it means poaching in national parks and game preserves. In addition, animals such as leopards, cheetahs, and crocodiles are hunted to supply fashionable furs and leather for export. Although elephants are no longer widely hunted for ivory, in the past they were slaughtered by the thousands for the sake of their tusks. Rhinos also have been killed for the supposed medicinal value of their horns. Finally, countless wild animals have been killed or captured for museum and zoo collections.

Fortunately for Africa's wildlife, however, worldwide attention and concern have encouraged the governments of the plains nations to recognize their unique natural treasures. Many threatened species are protected by vigorously enforced laws. National parks and game preserves have been established, many of them dedicated to the preservation of single species of endangered animals. The result has been the recovery of some of the rarest species, as well as the provision of sanctuaries for more common wild animals. Today, throughout the region, the visitor is certain to notice the enormous interest and pride of both government officials and ordinary citizens in the safeguarding of their wildlife.

Pictured below are several examples of African animals that are in special need of protection if they are to survive.

GIANT SABLE ANTELOPE
One of four subspecies of sable antelope, this handsome animal lives in a small area in central Angola, where it is legally protected in two reserves. Trophy hunters probably contributed to its decline to a population estimated at between 1000 and 2000 individuals. The greatest threat to its survival, however, is the destruction of its habitat by farmers who clear the land for shifting cultivation.

SWAYNE'S HARTEBEEST
The rarest of several subspecies of the common African hartebeest, Swayne's hartebeest originally lived in large herds in the Somali Republic and Ethiopia. Now it is extinct in the Somali Republic, a victim of epidemics of the disease rinderpest that swept Africa in the 1890s. Uncontrolled hunting also took its toll in Ethiopia, where only about 200 of these large antelopes survive in a few herds.

WESTERN GIANT ELAND

This rare subspecies of the giant eland, standing nearly six feet high at the shoulder, survives in extremely small numbers in a few scattered areas in Senegal, Mali, and Guinea. A victim of rinderpest and uncontrolled hunting, its future looks bleak unless the few dozen surviving individuals are given strict and immediate protection. Fortunately, the other two subspecies of the giant elands do not seem to be in danger of extinction.

BLACK WILDEBEEST

Early in this century, this animal was nearly exterminated by farmers for the sake of meat and hides, but strict protection in parks, in game preserves, and on private land has rescued it from the brink of extinction. Also called the white-tailed gnu, it is distinguished from the black wildebeest by its upward curving horns, the brushy hair on its face, the tufts on its throat and chest, and its long, flowing white tail.

MOUNTAIN ZEBRA

This smallest of zebras, standing only four feet high at the shoulders, is a resident of dry mountains and hills in South Africa. Settlement of the land, competition with domestic stock, and excessive hunting nearly exterminated the species early in the twentieth century. Even with strict protection in Mountain Zebra National Park and on a few private farms, however, the population in 1965 totaled only 75 animals.

Adaptation: An inherited structural, functional, or behavioral characteristic that improves an organism's chances for survival in a particular *habitat*.

Annual: A plant that completes its life cycle from seedling to mature seed-bearing plant during a single growing season, then dies. *See also* Perennial.

Antelope: Any of a group of fast-moving, cud-chewing, deerlike animals, usually bearing a pair of unbranched horns, belonging to the same family as goats and cows. Wildebeests, hartebeests, duikers, gazelles, and many other grazing animals of the African plains are antelope.

Boma: A Masai word for a thatch-roofed mud hut; boma may also refer to the fence built around a native village or animal pen for protection against wild animals. *See also* Manyatta.

Browser: An animal, such as a giraffe, that feeds primarily on the leaves, buds, and twigs of trees and shrubs. *See also* Grazer.

Bunch grass: The general term for types of grass that grow in separate, well-spaced tufts instead of creeping to form a solid mat of turf. Most of the grasses that grow on *savannas* are bunch grasses.

Carnivore: An animal such as a lion that lives by eating the flesh of other animals. *See also* Herbivore; Omnivore.

Carrion: The dead and decaying flesh of an animal.

Carrying capacity: The maximum number of individuals of a particular kind of animal that can be supported year-round within a given unit of *habitat*.

Climate: The average long-term *weather* conditions of an area, based on records kept for many years and including temperature, rainfall, humidity, windiness, and hours of sunlight.

Climatic savanna: A *savanna* resulting from special climatic conditions, with rainfall concentrated in six or eight months of the year, followed by a long period of drought.

Commensalism: A symbiotic relationship between two dissimilar organisms in which one of the partners benefits while the other is neither helped nor harmed. *See also* Mutualism; Symbiosis.

Competition: The struggle between individuals or groups of living things for such common necessities as food, water, or living space.

Conservation: The use of the earth's natural resources in a way that ensures their continuing availability to future generations; the wise use of natural resources.

Derived savanna: A *savanna* made by men when they clear forest land for *shifting cultivation*. After planting crops for a few years, the men abandon the clearings, allowing grass to take over before trees can become reestablished.

Display: An inherited behavior pattern, often involving elaborate posturing, movements, or other ritualized actions, by which animals communicate with others of the same species. Displays are usually associated with activities such as courtship and territorial defense.

Dominant: The most prevalent kind of plant or animal in a given habitat at a given time, usually the species best adapted for survival there.

Drought: A prolonged period when little or no moisture falls on an area.

Ecology: The science which studies the relationships of living things to each other and to their nonliving environment.

Edaphic savanna: A *savanna* resulting from certain soil conditions and not entirely maintained by fire.

Environment: All the external conditions, such as soil, water, air, and organisms, surrounding a living thing.

Equator: An imaginary circle around the middle of the earth, equally distant at all points from both the North and South Poles.

Erosion: The wearing away of areas of the earth's surface by water, wind, ice, and other natural forces.

Evolution: The process of natural consecutive modification in the inherited makeup of living things; the process by which modern plants and animals have arisen through adaptation and natural selection from more generalized forms that lived in the prehistoric past.

Fossil: Any remains or traces of animals or plants that lived in the prehistoric past, whether bone, cast, track, imprint, pollen, or any other evidence of their existence.

Game ranching: Managing herds of wild grazing animals in order to harvest part of their annual increase in numbers for human food.

Grass: Any plant distinguished by jointed, usually hollow stems, two-part leaves consisting of a sheath around the stem and a long flat blade, tiny flowers borne on small spikes, and dry seedlike fruits.

Grazer: An animal that feeds primarily on *grass*, such as a zebra or domestic cow. *See also* Browser.

Habitat: The immediate surroundings (living place) of a plant or animal; everything necessary to life in a particular location except the life itself.

Herbivore: An animal that eats plants. *See also* Carnivore; Omnivore.

Kopje: An Afrikaans term for a small hill, usually composed of smooth, rounded boulders.

Mammals: The group of animals including humans, bats, cattle, and many other forms. All are warm-blooded, possess special milk-producing glands, are at least partially covered with hair, and usually bear their young alive.

Manyatta: A Masai village site, including a cluster of *bomas* and the surrounding fence; manyatta can also refer to an enclosure for domestic animals.

Migration: A periodic, especially seasonal or annual, movement from one place to another of large numbers of a species of animal.

Mutualism: A symbiotic relationship between two dissimilar organisms in which both partners benefit. *See also* Commensalism; Symbiosis.

Omnivore: A mixed feeder; an animal whose normal diet includes both plants and animals. *See also* Carnivore; Herbivore.

Overgrazing: Excessive feeding on the vegetation of an area by wild or domestic animals, resulting in serious and often permanent damage to the area's ability to support desirable plant life.

222

Pantropical: Occurring around the world in tropical areas.

Pastoralist: A farmer who lives by tending herds or flocks of domestic animals.

Perennial: A plant that lives for several years and usually produces seeds each year. *See also* Annual.

Poacher: A person who hunts illegally for game.

Predator: An animal such as a leopard or cheetah that lives by capturing other animals for food. *See also* Prey.

Prey: A living animal that is captured for food by another animal. *See also* Predator.

Pride: A family or social group of lions.

Safari: A Swahili term for an extended journey or expedition; it may be for sightseeing, photography, or hunting.

Savanna: A grass-covered plain with widely spaced trees found in many areas of the tropics. Savannas usually are found where annual rainy seasons alternate with long periods of drought. During the dry season, the grass frequently burns as a result of natural or man-made fires which suppress the growth of most trees. *See also* Climatic savanna; Derived savanna; Edaphic savanna.

Scavenger: An animal such as a vulture that eats the dead remains and wastes of other animals and plants.

Shifting cultivation: A primitive method of farming in which clearings are made in the forest by felling and burning the trees, crops are planted for one or a few growing seasons, and then, when the soil loses its fertility, the plots are abandoned and new clearings are made elsewhere.

Shrub: A woody plant less than twelve feet tall, usually with more than one stem rising from the ground.

Sleeping sickness: A type of *trypanosomiasis* affecting human beings and transmitted by tsetse flies. The disease causes fever, inflammation of the brain, sleepiness, increasing weakness, and usually death.

Species (singular or plural): A group of plants or animals with many characteristics in common. Individuals belonging to the same species resemble each other more closely than they resemble individuals of any other species and usually interbreed with each other.

Standard livestock unit: The measure, equaling one thousand pounds of living animal, used by ranchers throughout the world to estimate the *carrying capacity* of their land. One healthy cow with a small calf is considered to be a standard livestock unit.

Standing crop biomass: The actual total weight of living matter, or of a specific kind of plant or animal, in a given area at a given time.

Subspecies (singular or plural): A group of individuals of the same *species* living within a more or less well-defined geographical area and differing slightly but consistently from individuals of the same species living elsewhere. A single species of plant or animal may include many subspecies.

Sucker: A shoot growing from an underground root.

Symbiosis: An association of two dissimilar organisms in a relationship that may benefit one or both partners. In the case of the symbiotic relationship called parasitism, one partner (the parasite) benefits, but the other (the host) is harmed by the association.

Telephoto lens: A photographic lens used to produce a large image of a distant object.

Territory: An area defended by an animal against others of the same species. A territory may be used for breeding, feeding, or both.

223

Tropic of Cancer: An imaginary circle around the earth 23.45 degrees north of the *equator*. It forms the northern boundary of the *tropics*.

Tropic of Capricorn: An imaginary circle around the earth 23.45 degrees south of the *equator*. It forms the southern boundary of the *tropics*.

Tropics: The area of the earth's surface lying between the *Tropic of Cancer* and the *Tropic of Capricorn*. The tropics are characterized by the absence of winter and, except at high altitudes, by constantly warm temperatures.

Trypanosomiasis: Any of several diseases caused by infection by trypanosomes, a group of minute parasitic protozoans that inhabit the blood stream, and transmitted by bloodsucking insects such as tsetse flies. African sleeping sickness is one type of trypanosomiasis.

Tuber: A fleshy or thickened underground stem, such as the edible portion of a potato plant.

Veldt: An Afrikaans term for open grazing land.

Water hole: Any more or less permanent standing pool of water on savanna, desert, or rangeland, whether natural or man-made.

Weather: The condition of the atmosphere over a relatively short period of time, in terms of temperature, humidity, windiness, presence or absence of precipitation, and clearness or cloudiness. *See also* Climate.

Wide-angle lens: A photographic lens that permits a relatively wide angle of view.

Wilderness: A tract of land, whether savanna, desert, forest, or any other, where man is only a visitor; an area where the original natural community of plants and animals survives in balance and intact, unaltered by mechanized civilization.

Bibliography

AFRICAN NATURAL HISTORY

AKELEY, CARL ETHAN. *In Brightest Africa*. Doubleday, 1923.

AMES, EVELYN. *A Glimpse of Eden*. Houghton Mifflin, 1967.

ASTLEY MABBERLY, C. T. *Animals of East Africa*. Hodder, 1966.

BARTLETT, JEN, and DES BARTLETT. *Nature's Paradise*. Houghton Mifflin, 1967.

BROWN, LESLIE. *Africa: A Natural History*. Random House, 1965.

BROWN, LESLIE. *Ethiopian Episode*. Country Life, 1965.

CARR, ARCHIE. *Ulendo: Travels of a Naturist in and out of Africa*. Knopf, 1964.

CARR, ARCHIE, and THE EDITORS OF LIFE. *The Land and Wildlife of Africa*. Time, Inc., 1964.

DARLING, F. FRAZER. *Wild Life in an African Territory*. Oxford University Press, 1960.

HALLET, JEAN-PIERRE, with ALEX PELLE. *Animal Kitabu*. Random House, 1965.

ISEMONGER, R. M. *Snakes of Africa*. Nelson, 1962.

MOOREHEAD, ALAN. *The White Nile*. Harper & Row, 1961.

O'LEARY, NIETER, and PAMELA PAULET. *African Wildlife*. Viking, 1965.

OWEN, D. F. *Animal Ecology in Tropical Africa*. Freeman, 1966.

SIMON, NOEL. *Between the Sunlight and the Thunder: The Wild Life of Kenya*. Houghton Mifflin, 1963.

SKAIFE, S. H. *African Insect Life*. Longmans, 1954.

SPINAGE, C. A. *Animals of East Africa*. Houghton Mifflin, 1963.

STEVENSON-HAMILTON, J. *Wild Life in South Africa*. Cassell, 1954.

MAMMALS

ADAMSON, JOY. *Born Free*. Pantheon, 1960.

CARRINGTON, RICHARD. *Elephants*. Basic Books, 1959.

COWIE, MERVYN. *I Walk with Lions*. Macmillan, 1964.

DOMINIS, JOHN, and MAITLAND EDEY. *The Cats of Africa*. Time, Inc., 1968.

DORST, JEAN, and PIERRE DANDELOT. *A Field Guide to the Larger Mammals of Africa*. Houghton Mifflin, 1970.

ELLERMAN, J. R., T. C. S. MORRISON-SCOTT, and R. W. HAYMAN. *Southern African Mammals*. British Museum, 1953.

SIKES, S. K. *The Natural History of the African Elephant*. American Elsevier, 1971.

VAN LAWICK-GOODALL, HUGO, and JANE VAN LAWICK-GOODALL, *Innocent Killers*. Houghton Mifflin, 1971.

BIRDS

BROWN, LESLIE. *African Birds of Prey*. Houghton Mifflin, 1971.

CAVE, FRANCIS O., and JAMES D. MACDONALD. *Birds of the Sudan*. Oliver & Boyd, 1955.

CLANCEY, P. A. *Gamebirds of Southern Africa*. American Elsevier, 1967.

MACKWORTH-PRAED, C. W., and C. H. B. GRANT. *Birds of Eastern and North Eastern Africa*. Longmans, 1957–1960.

MACKWORTH-PRAED, C. W., and C. H. B. GRANT. *Birds of the Southern Third of Africa*. Longmans, 1962–1963.

MOREAU, R. E. *Bird Faunas of Africa and Its Islands*. Academic, 1966.

WILLIAMS, JOHN G. *A Field Guide to the Birds of East and Central Africa*. Houghton Mifflin, 1964.

PLANTS

CHIPPINDALL, LUCY K. A., and others. *The Grasses and Pastures of South Africa*. Central News Agency (Johannesburg), 1955.

CODD, L. E. W. *Trees and Shrubs of the Kruger National Park*. Government Printer (Pretoria), 1951.

EDWARDS, D. C., and A. V. BOGDAN. *Important Grassland Plants of Kenya*. Pitman, 1951.

EGGELING, WILLIAM JULIUS. *The Indigenous Trees of Uganda*. Government Printer (Entebbe), 1940.

JEX-BLAKE, A. J. (Editor). *Gardening in East Africa*. Longmans, 1957.

LIND, E. M., and A. C. TALLANTIRE. *Some Common Flowering Plants of Uganda*. Oxford University Press, 1962.

PALMER, EVE, and NORAH PITMAN. *Trees of South Africa*. A. A. Balkema, 1961.

RATTRAY, J. M. *The Grass Cover of Africa*. Food and Agriculture Organization of the United Nations, 1960.

CONSERVATION

BEARD, PETER H. *The End of the Game*. Viking, 1965.

CULLEN, ANTHONY, and SYDNEY DOWNEY. *Saving the Game*. Jarrolds, 1960.

FISHER, JAMES, NOEL SIMON, and JACK VINCENT. *Wildlife in Danger*. Viking, 1969.

GRZIMEK, BERNHARD. *Serengeti Shall Not Die*. Dutton, 1961.

HUXLEY, JULIAN. *The Conservation of Wild Life and Natural Habitats in Central and East Africa*. UNESCO, 1961.

NICOL, C. W. *From the Roof of Africa*. Knopf, 1972.

PHILLIPS, JOHN. *Agriculture and Ecology in Africa*. Praeger, 1960.

WILLIAMS, JOHN G. *A Field Guide to the National Parks of East Africa*. Houghton Mifflin, 1968.

WILLOCK, C. *The Enormous Zoo: A Profile of the Uganda National Parks*. Harcourt, Brace & World, 1965.

Illustration Credits and Acknowledgments

COVER: Lion, John Flannery

ENDPAPERS: Mark Boulton, National Audubon Society

UNCAPTIONED PHOTOGRAPHS: 8–9: Grant's gazelles, Leonard Lee Rue III 60–61: Mixed herd, M. Philip Kahl 104–105: Lion with kill, George B. Schaller 158–159: Masai herder, Ed Degginger

ALL OTHER ILLUSTRATIONS: 10–11: Peter Fraenkel, Carl E. Ostman 12–13: Sally Anne Thompson, Scala 14: Emil Muench 15: Ed Degginger; Emil Muench 16: M. P. L. Fogden; George B. Schaller 17: Leonard Lee Rue III 18–19: George B. Schaller 21: Afrique Photo 22: George J. Chafaris 23: Emil Muench, Carl E. Ostman 24–25: Richard D. Estes 26–27: Afrique Photo 28: Norman Myers, Bruce Coleman, Inc. 29: Alan Root 30–31, 33: Richard D. Estes 34–35: Alan Root 36–37: M. Philip Kahl 38: Alan Root 39: Norman Myers, Bruce Coleman, Inc. 41: H. D. Kirk 42: Dale A. Zimmerman; K. B. Newman; Edward S. Ross 43: H. D. Kirk 44–45: Edward S. Ross 46: Leonard Lee Rue III 47–49: Alan Root 50–51: Patricia C. Henrichs 52: R. Woodford 53: Norman Myers, Bruce Coleman, Inc. 54–55: Sally Anne Thompson, Scala 57: Harold Faye 58: Richard D. Estes 62–65: Alan Root 66: Tex Fuller 67: J. Cannon, Carl E. Ostman 68–69: Patricia C. Henrichs 70: Leonard Lee Rue III 72: M. P. L. Fogden; Des Bartlett, Bruce Coleman, Inc. 73: Edward S. Ross 75: Leslie Brown 76: M. Philip Kahl; Norman Lightfoot 77: Norman Myers, Bruce Coleman, Inc. 78: Leonard Lee Rue III 79: Peter Johnson 80–81: Norman Myers, Bruce Coleman, Inc. 82: Mark Boulton, National Audubon Society 83: J. Allan Cash 84: M. Philip Kahl 85: Ed Degginger 86–87 Alan Root 88: Afrique Photo 89: Charles Fracé 90: Matthew Kalmenoff 91–93: Emil Muench, Carl E. Ostman 94: Alan Root 96–97: George B. Schaller 98: Mark Boulton 99: Afrique Photo 100: Leonard Lee Rue III 101: Matthew Kalmenoff 102: Leonard Lee Rue III 106: George B. Schaller 107: M. Philip Kahl 108–109: Bob Campbell, Bruce Coleman, Inc. 110: Charles Fracé 111–114: Alan Root 115: Sally Anne Thompson, Scala 116: Alan Root 118: C. G. Hampson 119: George

B. Schaller 120–121: Tex Fuller 123: Leonard Lee Rue III 124–125: Tex Fuller 126: George B. Schaller 127: Norman Myers, Bruce Coleman, Inc. 128–129: Peter Ward 130: Norman Myers, Bruce Coleman, Inc. 131: Leonard Lee Rue III 132: Charles Fracé 133: Weldon King, Free Lance Photographer's Guild, Inc. 134–135: Charles Fracé 136: Richard D. Estes 137–139: Alan Root 140–141: Mark Boulton 142: Thase Daniel 144: Peter Johnson 145: Alan Root 146: Peter Johnson 147: Matthew Kalmenoff 148: K. B. Newman 149: Thase Daniel 150: Peter Johnson 151: Patricia C. Henrichs 152: Alan Root 153: John Flannery 154–155: Afrique Photo 156: George B. Schaller 160–161: J. Allan Cash 162–163: George B. Schaller 164: K. B. Newman 165: R. M. Bradley 166–167: Matthew Kalmenoff 168–171: Jen & Des Bartlett, Bruce Coleman, Inc. 173: Norman Myers, Bruce Coleman, Inc. 174–175: Emil Muench, Carl E. Ostman 176–177: Leonard Lee Rue III; J. R. Simon, Carl E. Ostman 178–179: M. Philip Kahl 180–181: F. W. Taylor & Co. 182–183: M. Philip Kahl 184–185: Patricia C. Henrichs 186–187: Emil Muench; M. Philip Kahl 188: Sally Anne Thompson, Scala 189–190: Afrique Photo 191: M. Philip Kahl 192–193: J. Allan Cash 194: Norman Lightfoot 195: Patricia C. Henrichs 196: Thase Daniel 197: M. P. L. Fogden 198: John Flannery 201: Charles Fracé 203–209: Patricia C. Henrichs 210: Graphic Arts International 211–212: Patricia C. Henrichs 213–220: Charles Fracé

PHOTO EDITOR: Barbara Knowlton

ACKNOWLEDGMENTS: *It is impossible to acknowledge the assistance of everyone who contributed to the preparation of this volume, but several persons deserve special thanks. The publishers are especially grateful to C. Gordon Fredine, of the National Park Service, for reading the entire manuscript and offering several useful suggestions. For their critical reviews of portions of the manuscript, the author would like to thank Keith Eltringham of the Nuffield Unit of Tropical Animal Ecology at Queen Elizabeth National Park, Uganda; Hans Kruuk of the Serengeti Research Institute at Serengeti National Park, Tanzania; and Richard Leakey of the National Museum of Kenya.*

Index

228